# Play! Think! Grow!
## 234 Activities for Christian Growth

# Contents

# Contents: Topics

# and Activities

# Teaching Christian Values to Young Children

Because we are Christian, we want to teach Christian values to the young children in our charge. But exactly what do we mean by Christian values and how do we teach them?

In the New Testament we find many values discussed both in the letters of Paul and in the Gospels. Jesus summarized them all in his response to the Pharisee who asked which commandment was the greatest. "[Jesus] said to him, 'You shall love the Lord your God with all your heart, and with all your soul, and with all your mind.' This is the greatest and first commandment. And a second is like it: 'You shall love your neighbor as yourself.' On these two commandments hang all the law and the prophets" (Matthew 22:37-40).

What do Jesus' words mean for children and for us as their teachers and caregivers? How can we help children love God and love others?

## Activities Teach Values

The concepts of loving God and of loving others need to be concrete and specific for young children. We want them to learn to share, to take turns, to be helpful to others, to be considerate of others, to take care of things at school and at home, to work hard at tasks, to reach beyond themselves to those in need, to have reverence for God and respect for creation, and to show kindness to friends and family.

How can we use activities to help children learn these values? Young children learn best through experience and by doing. Those attitudes and practices that we know well were learned through experience and practice.

**Sharing.** Well-equipped rooms for young children provide many materials, but the toys and equipment—even the attention of caregivers—are meant for children to share. The art table, the home living center, blocks, and laps provide opportunities for children to learn the pleasure of sharing.

**Taking turns.** Children learn to take turns. They learn that they are important persons, and that they will get a turn. They discover that others in the classroom are important too and deserve their turn as well.

**Being helpful.** Children can do simple tasks for the class. Each one can take a turn helping to set out things for snack time or holding the door as the class goes outside to play. Children soon enjoy helping a friend put on his or her coat or simply handing a toy to a playmate.

**Caring for the materials.** While many activities in preschool classes can be messy, the children know that when the class finishes an activity, they and the teacher will clean the room. Equipment for young children is sturdy and designed to withstand hands-on learning, but teachers help children use those materials wisely. Teachers set up the room so children can get out materials and put them away by themselves. As the children learn to care for materials in the room, they develop responsibility and independence.

**Enhancing self-esteem.** Sometimes parents worry whether their children will learn to work at a task until finished. Teachers can allow children to make choices among activities and then give them time and opportunity to work at that activity until they complete the task. Sometimes a child who is struggling to figure out how to do a puzzle will ask the teacher for help. A wise teacher offers support and suggestions so the child can see how to solve the puzzle but does not solve it for the child. In letting children work through the problem, the teacher allows children to stick with a task and to feel good about what they can do.

That same wise teacher will plan the class schedule so that the child working on an art activity, in the block center, or pretending in the home living center has time to work through difficulties on his or her own. Children need to have time to try several solutions to a problem.

**Reaching out to others.** Young children can participate in efforts at church to help others. Through experiencing the love of others at church and home, children are then able to reach out to others.

With the encouragement of teachers, children learn to reach out to a friend or classmate with sympathy or care. Collecting books or school supplies for children who need them and visiting persons who are lonely and confined to their home offer opportunities for children to reach out to others.

**Valuing others.** A very important part of respecting all of God's creation is learning to respect the worth of every living person. We want to teach young children that persons of every race and culture are of value even if they seem to be different or look different. We also want young children to learn to accept handicapped persons as persons of worth.

In early childhood programs, teachers can give children experiences with real persons and with books and pictures that include all kinds of persons.

**Caring for God's earth.** Nature activities such as planting seeds and watching them grow, observing a beautiful monarch butterfly that develops from a worm into an uninteresting-looking chrysalis, and going on a listening or smelling walk can all contribute to the development of an attitude of awe and respect for all of life.

In the classroom children may become aware of the importance of reusing as many materials as possible. Since so many of the materials we use in teaching young children are recycled, children learn from experience how to use things more than one way. They can learn to help save things at home to use in class.

**Activities Promote Christian Values**

Activities are important for promoting Christian values. However, activities themselves are not enough. Two other factors come into play: relationships and climate.

Donald Rogers, a Christian educator, says that activities in the curriculum are simply the means by which teachers have a relationship with children (*Children and Faith*, videotape; Graded Press). The appropriate activities are important, but they are only tools for teaching. The relationship between the teacher and the children is primary.

At the same time, a teacher who cares about the children will create a warm, loving climate for the class. A caring teacher will provide activities for young children that allow them to be who they are—to be who God created them to be at that age. Then the children will feel accepted as they are and want to be like the teacher and do the things that the teacher communicates are important. Teachers teach Christian values within the loving environment they create, using activities the children will enjoy.

Sometimes we who are caregivers and teachers do not realize we are communicating values. *How* we do the activities is as important as *what* we do. The teacher's relationships with the children and the classroom climate model Christian values as much or more than do the activities offered.

Children are learning all the time. They are learning values from everything that happens to them and from everything they observe. They learn from the things we plan as well as from things we never think about.

God calls us as adults to continue to grow in our own faith, to continue to learn how to love God and to love others. From our own maturing faith we present good role models for the children. As we seek to do these things, we are teaching Christian values.

# Developing a Child's Self-esteem

Jesus said, "Love your neighbor as yourself." Many times we hear this verse used to remind us to love our neighbors, but it is also a very powerful lesson about the importance of self-esteem. The verse is telling us that we cannot love anyone until we love ourselves. So self-love is essential for the development of loving persons in our world, because if we do not love ourselves, we cannot love others.

The early years of children's lives are critical to the development of their self-concept. Whether they see themselves as worthy of love and capable of doing well is determined by how they are treated by parents, grandparents, teachers, and caregivers in the first five years of life. While parents have the most profound effect on children's self-esteem, those of us who care for and teach young children also play a very important part in building a positive self-concept in children.

It is very important that we evaluate all our procedures and our language—both verbal and body—to determine if we are building children's self-esteem. Our goal should be to help children develop strong self-esteem so that they will grow into adults who know that they are lovable and capable and can function in society as contributing adults.

## How to Build Self-Esteem in Children

Building self-esteem is a process that permeates everything we do in the classroom. What kind of things can teachers do with children that will enhance their self-esteem?

• *Teachers build self-esteem when they are ready as the children arrive in the morning and greet the children with a smile.* Then children begin the day feeling accepted just the way they are. They can begin the day ready for new experiences.

• *Teachers build self-esteem when they set up the classroom so that children can make choices about their activities.* Having a choice communicates to the children that they are capable persons whom the teacher trusts to make good choices.

• *Teachers build self-esteem when they plan age-appropriate activities that children can do themselves.* If teachers present an art activity that is too difficult for the children to do by themselves, the children feel there is

> *The early years of children's lives are critical to the development of their self-concept. Whether they see themselves as worthy of love and capable of doing well is determined by how they are treated...*

something wrong with them because they cannot do what the teacher has asked. If the teacher does some of the work, the child feels that his or her efforts are not good enough and may feel discouraged about trying the next new thing that the teacher suggests.

• *Teachers build self-esteem when they remember that most learning goes on when children do self-directed activities.* This principle requires that children spend much less time listening in the total group or listening to the teacher and more time in center activities. Young children are active persons with short attention spans who learn best by doing.

• *Teachers build self-esteem when they speak positively to children.* Avoid the use of the words "no" and "don't" as much as possible when talking to young children.

• *Teachers build self-esteem when they use appropriate guidance methods.* Children are taught how to behave rather than being punished for behaving in improper ways.

• *Teachers build self-esteem when they take time to sit and talk with children.* Listen with interest to what the children say. Smile and say the children's names often and reaffirm what the child is telling you.

• *Teachers build self-esteem when they encourage individuality.* At nap time, for instance, does one child take off her dress when she goes to sleep, while another has to have that special blanket, and a third doesn't want to take off his new shoes?

A teacher who builds self-esteem will allow individual differences that do not bother other persons rather than requiring all the children to do the same thing the same way.

• *Teachers build self-esteem when children are praised for their accomplishments.* Encourage children to keep trying when they are learning a new skill. Give genuine praise to children who deserve it.

• *Teachers build self-esteem when they understand that learning to share is a long process.* Children need much time, practice, and understanding to accomplish this goal.

• *Teachers build self-esteem when they give children opportunities to cooperate, to help, and to negotiate.* Children then feel that they are important and that what they think matters.

**Values of Strong Self-esteem**

Persons who have strong self-esteem are capable of giving and helping others because they know they are valuable persons. They do not have to keep calling attention to themselves in some way because they don't feel good about themselves.

1. Persons with strong self-esteem have the courage to try new things and to try again when something doesn't work.
2. Persons with strong self-esteem are hard to lead astray. They know who they are and usually know where they are going.
3. Persons with strong self-esteem know that God always loves them. They know that they are not perfect and that they are always growing, but they also know that they are loved and accepted by God and others.

As Christian teachers of young children, we should place the development of positive self-concept first among our teaching goals. If our students feel good about themselves, they will become effective functioning persons in God's world.

# Maintaining a Safe and Healthy Environment

Health and safety are subjects that teachers often take for granted. Sometimes we do not emphasize practices that will promote health and safety because it may be inconvenient or is not important to learning.

**Tips for Hand Washing**

The most important health practice for young children is hand washing. Children should wash their hands before they eat and after they use the toilet. Hands should be washed in running water with soap. The soap should be lathered and thoroughly spread over the hands and up the arms.

Caregivers who change diapers must be careful to wash their hands before and after every diaper change. Diarrhea and other diseases can be easily spread through germs on the caregivers' hands.

**Helps for Good Nutrition**

Good nutrition is an investment that pays off in many ways:
1. Children feel better because they have not had too much sugar or fat.
2. When children feel well, their behavior is much more appropriate.
3. Some children's bodies react to artificial colors and flavors.
4. Children will develop eating habits that promote health.

**Exercise for Good Health**

Give children opportunities to use large and small muscles daily. The playground provides some large-muscle exercise, but supplement outdoor play with indoor climbing, riding wheel toys, or playing running games.

Creative movement allows children to jump, hop, skip, crawl, or stretch. Marching to music, and later marching and playing instruments together, provides fun exercise.

Small muscles are developed through putting together manipulative toys, doing creative art projects, playing with play dough, or using scissors or crayons.

**Set the Emotional Tone**

Part of a healthy environment includes the emotional tone of the group. Teachers should keep their voices low and use appropriate guidance techniques when needed. Plan room arrangements and schedules to limit the need to correct children's behavior. The emotional tone of a classroom for young children should be relaxed and warm. When the emotional tone is appropriate, self-esteem is promoted and everyone learns better.

**Plan for Safety**

Teachers may limit children's behavior to ensure their safety. Possible hazards in rooms and play space used by the children may occur from lack of good maintenance of buildings and equipment. Teachers should report needed repairs and remove the equipment from the room until repairs are made.

Supervision is very important. Most accidents happen when teachers are not adequately supervising a child or group of children. Lack of supervision can happen when teachers become involved in changing diapers and do not see what the other children are doing.

Health and safety concerns are basic to a quality program. Each child is a child of God and of great worth. Each child deserves a safe, healthy environment in our church's programs.

# Creating an Inviting Environment

Have you ever noticed what affects your feelings when you go into a new place such as a doctor's office or a school or a church? The colors, the type of furniture and its arrangement, and the pictures on the walls or the lack of them are among the things that affect the way you feel.

When children come into your room, how do they feel? Does your room welcome them? Does it invite them to come in and explore?

As you plan for your class, you need to consider not only individual activities but also the learning environment.

Everything from the colors on the walls, to the arrangement of the furniture, to the schedule of time affects the behavior and the learning of the children.

Sometimes teachers try to brighten up dingy rooms by adding color to the walls, but sometimes we can overpower a small room with too much color.

This was the case in a small classroom that had one long wall painted red and no carpet on the floor. Teachers complained that the children in the room were uncontrollable. When the director went into the room, she wanted to shout because of the stimulation of the color. Her urge to shout was reinforced by the lack of soft materials that soaked up sound. So when she did shout, she was rewarded by a wonderful echo. No wonder the children were all overstimulated!

In a group of toddlers, there was always someone crying. A teacher observing in the room noticed that there was no soft cozy place for the children to cuddle down and be quiet or to practice comforting themselves. So when the children needed some comfort, they followed the teacher around and cried to be picked up.

When the teacher wanted to gather all the crying children around her and cuddle up, there was no place except a small corner of the carpet near the slide in the center of the room.

**Prepare Your Environment**

The environment itself will affect the way the children in your class behave. Teachers must be aware of these subtle factors in order to create a learning environment that is welcoming, comfortable, and yet stimulating.

*Room Surfaces*

Rooms should contain both hard and soft surfaces. Surfaces for art should be hard and washable, but a book corner should have a rug and perhaps a large pillow. Soft surfaces are necessary to absorb sound and to provide a soft, cuddling space.

*Room Colors*

Color should be in the equipment and materials rather than on the walls. The books, puzzles, manipulatives, and dress-up clothes should have the color. Walls should ideally be a soft neutral color such as white with a touch of brown.

*Room Arrangement*

It is said that rooms speak. Be aware of what your room says to the children who come into it. You can get in touch with how your children see your room by kneeling at the doorway of your room and looking in.

• Do centers and open shelves invite children to come in and choose an activity?

• Are all the toys put out of sight so that children get the feeling that this is a place in which the teacher is in control and the

> *Everything from the colors on the walls, to the arrangement of the furniture, to the schedule of time affects the behavior and the learning of the children.*

children are not allowed activity without permission?

• Are the pictures at the children's or the adult's eye level?

• Are there so many decorations that a child cannot tell if the class will talk about dinosaurs or Easter this week?

• Are there large open spaces that invite the children to run? Position storage shelves or other equipment so that they extend into the room. They mark the boundaries of centers and discourage running.

• Did you leave a large enough space to have together time for your class?

• Are other centers defined so that children know what activities are appropriate in that space?

• Is your book center in a quiet, relatively undisturbed part of the room?

• Do you have a water supply close to the creative art center?

• Can you place the family living center and the building center near one another so that children can use the resources in both of these centers?

### Equipment and Supplies

Rooms that are arranged neatly and simply in centers with equipment and materials displayed on open shelves or in labeled containers say that children have choices, that they are respected for their abilitites, and that they are growing in independence and responsibility.

Teachers reinforce these values when they plan a schedule that allows the children plenty of time to work in centers following their own interests.

### You Are Responsible

The basic room arrangement for preschool children includes four centers. While rooms for fours and fives might include more than these, they would still offer the basic four. The four are

> building center
> book, puzzle, and manipulative center
> family living center
> creative art center

Prepare the environment as if you were planning a party. Be ready and available to the children as they arrive, and help them find an interesting activity with which to begin the day.

God has placed us in an orderly world that invites us to explore and to be creative. People have been charged with taking care of God's world and using its resources responsibly. When teachers create an inviting, appropriate learning environment, they help young children develop a biblically based attitude about the larger environment.

**Ages 3–6**

# Special Guest Day

*Children will show kindness by having a special thank you for an invited guest.*

*Christian Values:* showing love and kindness; appreciating talents of each person
*Bible:* Galatians 5:14 (You shall love your neighbor as yourself.)

## MATERIALS NEEDED

wallpaper sample books
children's scissors
special snack foods

## GETTING READY

- Let children compose and send an invitation to your guest (storyteller, carpenter, grandparent) in advance.
- Cut wallpaper into rectangles, at least 10 inches by 15 inches.
- Use a dark marking pen to draw a line 2 inches in from each edge of paper.

## HOW TO DO IT

- Fringe the edges of the wallpaper place mats. (Make one for the guest.)
- Let children serve a snack to the guest.
- Write a thank-you prayer to say before the snack.

## VARIATIONS

- *For younger children:* Scribble draw on paper to create their place mats.
- Make this a special event each month.

## HOW DID IT GO?

- Do the children need to practice cutting?

# Greeting Card Puzzles

*Children will discover symbols and traditions of holidays.*

**Christian Values:** enjoying celebrations; discovering sense of community

**Bible:** Psalm 118:24 (This is the day that God has made.)

## MATERIALS NEEDED

used greeting cards for various celebrations and holidays
adhesive paper
scissors

## GETTING READY
- Laminate cards with adhesive paper.
- Cut cards into two or three simple pieces—more pieces for older children.

## HOW TO DO IT
- Use puzzles during small-group play.
- Give each child pieces of several cards and put them together during circle time.

## VARIATIONS
- *For younger children:* Have greeting cards to look at, open up, and talk about.
- Drop the cards through a mailbox slot.

## HOW DID IT GO?
- Did the children recognize all of the holiday symbols?
- Could they talk about the holiday and their families?

# Brother/Sister Celebration

## MATERIALS NEEDED

- large chart tablet
- 7 inches of wide ribbon per child
- picture of each child
- 3-inch circles of posterboard
- markers
- safety pins
- masking tape

*Children will affirm their new role in the family after a baby is born by celebrating their own growth.*

*Christian Values:* enhancing self-esteem; caring for family members
*Bible:* James 2:15-16 (We are to care for other people.)

## GETTING READY

- Glue the child's picture on the circle of posterboard. Print "I AM A BIG _____" around the top. Print on the ribbon "I can show love." Glue to button and attach a safety pin.

## HOW TO DO IT

- Think of ways to show love to babies.
- Write a Celebration Litany.
  Example: _____ can help get things for Mom.
  Response: We are glad, God.
- Give the child the ribbon to wear.

## VARIATIONS

- *For younger children:* Roleplay ways to care for a baby.

## HOW DID IT GO?

- Did the child feel good about his or her new place in the family?
- Does the child have a postive self-image?

**SOCIAL-EMOTIONAL RELATIONSHIPS**

# A Birthday Celebration

*Children will affirm each other's birthdays and what they can do.*

*Christian Values:* emphasizing God's plan for growth; enhancing self-esteem

*Bible:* Luke 2:40 (Children grow today as Jesus grew.)

## MATERIALS NEEDED

flannelboard
colored pieces of felt
a birthday button

## GETTING READY
- Make felt cake and candles.
- Gather children closely around the flannelboard.
- Place felt cake on the flannelboard.

## HOW TO DO IT
- The class repeats together:
  "We have a birthday to celebrate,
So put the candles on the cake.
How many candles do you need?"
  (Birthday child responds and places felt candles on the cake.)
- Everyone counts the candles and then sings "Happy Birthday."
- Let birthday child wear the button.

## VARIATIONS
- *For younger children:* Reinforce the concept of how old they are.
- *For older children:* Learn the month and day of their birthday on the calendar.

## HOW DID IT GO?
- Did the child feel special and affirmed?

**SOCIAL-EMOTIONAL RELATIONSHIPS • MATH READINESS**

## MATERIALS NEEDED

yarn cut in necklace-sized
  pieces
tooth-shape pattern
white construction paper
18- by 22-inch tagboard
instant camera
paper punch

# Happy Toothday

*Children will feel special as they pass the milestone of losing a tooth.*

**Christian Values:** appreciating God's plan for growth and change in our bodies
**Bible:** Luke 2:40 (Children grow today as Jesus grew.)

## GETTING READY

• Make a large chart in the shape of a tooth. At the bottom print "I Am Growing. Thank you, God." At the top write "Lost Tooth Club."

## HOW TO DO IT

• When a child loses a tooth, he or she becomes a member of the tooth club. Give the child the tooth pattern to trace on construction paper.
• Let the child cut out the tooth. Write the child's name on it.
• Punch two holes at the top of the tooth and string the tooth on a necklace.
• Take a picture of the child smiling. Add it to the tooth club chart and write the child's name below the picture.

## VARIATIONS

• Encourage children to keep their tooth necklace and bring it to class each time they lose a tooth.

## HOW DID IT GO?

• Do the children appreciate God's plan for growth?
• Does this activity help children who may feel self-conscious?

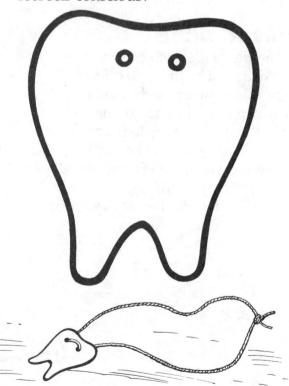

# Love One Another Mural

*Children will be reminded of Jesus' commandment "Love one another."*

*Christian Values:* appreciating those who show love for one another

*Bible:* 1 John 4:7 (Love one another.)

## MATERIALS NEEDED

long sheet of computer paper or shelf paper
red construction paper
scissors
felt-tip pen
glue sticks
masking tape
crayons

## GETTING READY
- Tape the computer paper onto the wall at the children's eye level.
- Cut one big heart from red construction paper, write "Love one another" on it, and glue it to the mural.
- Divide sheets of red construction paper into fourths. Fold each quarter in half and draw half a heart on it.

## HOW TO DO IT
- Talk about the different people the children love and ways the children show love.
- Give each child a folded half heart to cut out.
- Let children draw a picture on the heart of someone they love. Help them write that person's name.
- Glue the pictures on the mural.
- Thank God for the people the children love.

## VARIATIONS
- *For younger children:* Cut out a string of white paper dolls holding hands. Let the children decorate them.
- Glue the dolls onto red construction paper. Help the children write "Love one another."

## HOW DID IT GO?
- Were children able to talk about the people they love?
- Did they recognize ways of showing love?

Use w/
"Love Other People"
in childrens
Bible -
pg. 88
& "A Friend Loves"
song - pg. 163. music

## MATERIALS NEEDED

white construction paper
markers

# Action Prayer

*Children will affirm themselves and thank God by acting out a prayer.*

*Christian Values:* responding to God with gratitude; affirming self
*Bible:* Psalm 34:1 (I will always thank God.)

## GETTING READY
• Think about the different ways to pray. Find out how children pray at home.

## HOW TO DO IT
• Tell children they will pray in a different way today.
• Talk about the different parts of their body and what they can do (hands clap, mouths eat, feet walk).
• Lead and repeat the children's responses:
  My hands can clap (clap your hands)
  My feet can walk (walk in place)
  My mouth can sing (sing a short ditty)
• At the end all of you say "Thank you, God, for me."

## VARIATIONS
• *For older children:* Invite them to draw a picture of themselves and write "Thank you, God, for me."
• Use the prayer at different times during the year.

## HOW DID IT GO?
• Did the children sense that there are different ways of praying?
• How can you encourage the parents to pray with their children at home?

# Coffee Filter Butterflies

*Children will express appreciation for the beauty that God has created in butterflies.*

**Christian Values:** using God's gift of creativity; appreciating God's gift of butterflies
**Bible:** Psalm 16:9 (We are thankful and glad.)

## MATERIALS NEEDED

one coffee filter per child
one pipe cleaner per child
food coloring or tempera paints
small bowls for each color

## GETTING READY
- Fill bowls about one-third full of water.
- Put a few drops of coloring into each bowl.

## HOW TO DO IT
- Fold the coffee filter three or four times.
- Hold filter in the center and dip one corner into the colored water.
- Continue dipping each corner into a different color. Observe the colors blend.
- When the filter is dry, unfold it and twist it in the middle to form two wings. Wrap a pipe cleaner around the center. Twist the ends of the cleaner to form the antennae.

## VARIATIONS
- Glue some magnetic tape on the back and use to decorate the refrigerator for Mother's Day.

## HOW DID IT GO?
- Did the children express wonder and pride in their creation?

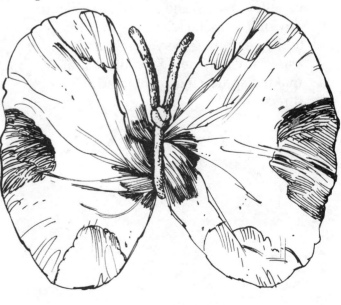

## MATERIALS NEEDED

a box filled with buttons,
   bits of lace, sequins,
   feathers, large and small
   bits of fabric, and so on
paper
glue
scissors

# Exploration Box

*Children will feel free to experiment and be creative by using the materials in the box on their free play time.*

**Christian Values:** appreciating God's gift of creativity; making choices
**Bible:** Genesis 1:27 (God made us with the ability to be creative.)

## GETTING READY
- Collect all kinds of glittery bits of odds and ends and place them in a box.
- Contents need to be changed periodically.

## HOW TO DO IT
- Explain to the children that the box contains materials to make pictures, collages, masks, and so on. They can use any of it to make whatever they like.
- In the beginning the younger children especially may not feel confident in making something without adult direction.

## VARIATIONS
- *For younger children:* When children are working, watch the twos and threes especially, to keep them from putting the objects in their mouth.
- *For older children:* They will enjoy creating banners, greeting cards, butterflies, puppets, or decorations for a party.

## HOW DID IT GO?
- How did you use or display the children's free creations?
- Did the children feel free to create without adult direction?

# Fancy Feet Collage

*Children will learn the sound of letter F by making a fancy feet collage.*

**Christian Values:** enhancing self-esteem; developing God's gift of learning
**Bible:** Genesis 1:26-28 (God made us with the ability to think and learn.)

## MATERIALS NEEDED

drawing paper
markers
*F* items: pieces of foil, funny papers, feathers, felt, flower pictures, foam
glue

## GETTING READY
- Place all *F* items in containers at the work area.
- Gather supplies.

## HOW TO DO IT
- Trace each child's feet with a marker.
- Identify the collage pieces as objects that start with the sound of *F*. Ask children to listen as you slowly say the words. Have children say names of objects.
- Let children glue the *F* objects inside their feet shapes.

## VARIATIONS
- *For older children:* Make footprints by dipping the child's bare feet in a shallow pan of tempera paint. Have the child step onto the paper; then into a pan of soapy water to clean the feet. Dry the feet.

## HOW DID IT GO?
- Did the children take pride in their feet creations?
- Could they identify the sound of *F*?

## MATERIALS NEEDED

tempera paints
paintbrushes
art paper
paint aprons
newspapers

# Flowers at Hand

*Children will enjoy turning their own hand and fist prints into flowers.*

**Christian Values:** using God's gift of creativity; praising God for beauty
**Bible:** Song of Solomon 2:12 (The flowers appear on the earth.)

## GETTING READY
- Show pictures of flowers.
- Cover a table with newspaper or cloth.
- Make sure children have on smocks or aprons.

## HOW TO DO IT
- Using one child at a time, paint the child's palm with tempera paint.
- Help the child place the palm in the middle of the paper.
- Continue making palm prints until there are three or four on the paper.
- After the painting dries, have the children add stems and leaves with green crayons or paint.
- Thank God for the gift of creativity.

## VARIATIONS
- *For younger children:* Paint long stems first; let dry. Have various colors of paints ready. Have a child dip finger tips in various colors of paint. Touch finger tips along each side of the stems to make pussy willows.
- *For older children:* Paint the outside of the fist to make a different shaped flower. Encourage children to move their hand sideways, in a circular motion, or up and down to create new designs.

## HOW DID IT GO?
- Did you notice that the children's self-esteem was enhanced through this project?

# Hearts in Our Hands

*Children will feel love as they create hearts using their hands.*

*Christian Values:* developing creativity;
developing self-esteem
*Bible:* John 15:17 (Love one another.)

## MATERIALS NEEDED

red or pink tempera paint
art paper
paint smocks
felt-tip marker
newspapers

## GETTING READY
- Cover a table with newspaper to protect the surface.
- Help children put on paint smocks.
- Write child's name on paper before painting.

## HOW TO DO IT
- Let a child paint both palms of another child with pink or red paint.
- Have a teacher place a piece of art paper in front of the child with painted palms. Then carefully press the child's hands on the paper palms down, thumb and index finger touching, wrists slightly apart.
- Allow paint to dry. If the painting is turned upside down, it resembles a heart shape!

## VARIATIONS
- *For older children:* Let children trace their hands on red or pink construction paper. Then cut out their handprints and arrange them into a heart shape.
- Use paper doilies, ribbon, or other art materials to enhance the hearts.
- Add a special loving message to the heart, or fold the art paper to make a greeting card. Give to a special friend.

## HOW DID IT GO?
- Could the children see the heart shape that was made?
- Did it make the children feel special to use their own hands to make a heart?

## MATERIALS NEEDED

large cardboard box
glue
markers
magazine covers
scissors
song "Jack-in-the-Box"

# Jack-in-the-Box

*Children will create something new from discarded materials to use in acting out a new song.*

*Christian Values:* caring for God's world; using God's gift of creativity
*Bible:* Genesis 1:28 (God asks us to take care of our world.)

## GETTING READY
• Talk about recycling and how we can make new things from something discarded.
• Gather brightly colored magazine covers and other supplies.

## HOW TO DO IT
• Children may decorate the cardboard box with snips cut or torn from the magazine covers. Decorate all four sides.
• Use with the song "Jack-in-the-Box."
• Let some children dramatize the rhyme as others sing the song. Children can curl up inside the box and jump out at the appropriate time.

## VARIATIONS
• Use the words to the song as a chant.
• See page 107 for directions to make a pop-up jack-in-the-box.

## HOW DID IT GO?
• Are the children more aware of the word *recycle*?
• Did they show pride in the box they decorated?

### Jack-in-the-Box

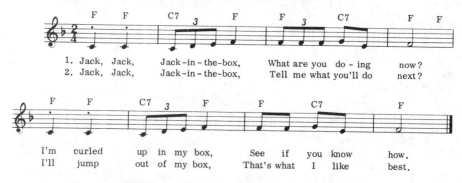

1. Jack, Jack, Jack-in-the-box, What are you do-ing now?
2. Jack, Jack, Jack-in-the-box, Tell me what you'll do next?

I'm curled up in my box, See if you know how.
I'll jump out of my box, That's what I like best.

WORDS and MUSIC: Elizabeth Parker © 1975 by Graded Press

# Rainy Day Fun

Children will discover fun on a rainy day by using art and nature to make something beautiful.

**Christian Values:** appreciating creativity and the wonder of God's creation
**Bible:** Psalm 104:13 (God sends rain from the sky.)

## MATERIALS NEEDED

coffee filter papers
water-color markers
rain (or water spray
 bottles)

## GETTING READY
- Identify an outdoor location where the project could be placed in the rain. You may alternatively use water in a spray bottle.

## HOW TO DO IT
- Let children decorate flattened filters with colored markers.
- Lay the filters in a light, misty rain, or let the children spray them lightly with water.
- Enjoy watching the colors blend and bleed to create new designs.

## VARIATIONS
- *For younger children:* Fill a flat baking pan with water. Use a medicine dropper to put one drop of water at a time into the pan. Watch the circles expand.
- *For older children:* Put your raincoats on and explore the beauty of raindrops in puddles of water. Observe the unique patterns each drop creates.
- Encourage children to make arm movements imitating the circles.

## HOW DID IT GO?
- Did the children respond with awe and wonder to the blending of colors?

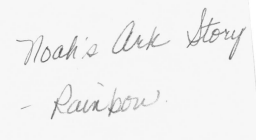

Noah's Ark Story
— Rainbow.

## MATERIALS NEEDED

baby-food jars with lids
white sand
tempera paint powder
cotton balls
small spoons
newspaper

# Sand Paperweights

*Children will have an opportunity to express friendship and to share with others.*

**Christian Values:** showing kindness; completing a task

**Bible:** 1 Corinthians 16:14 (Let all that you do be done in love.)

## GETTING READY
- Wash and dry jars thoroughly.
- Divide sand into several small plastic bags. Dampen slightly. Add a different color of paint to each bag. Shake bags until sand is evenly colored.
- Spread the colored sand on newspaper in the sun until thoroughly dry.

## HOW TO DO IT
- Give each child a jar. Children will choose colors of sand and spoon the sand into their jar making colorful layers or patterns.
- When the jar is full, pack cotton tightly on top and screw the lid securely on each jar. The packed cotton holds sand in place so that the colors won't mix when the jar is moved.

## VARIATIONS
- Use a large jar and make this a class project.
- Let children drizzle white glue on art paper and sprinkle colored sand on the glue to make a sand painting.

## HOW DID IT GO?
- Could children identify someone to whom they would like to give this gift?

# Wind Chimes

*Children will become aware of the wind and of God's plan for the earth.*

*Christian Values:* appreciating God's creation; recognizing the interdependence of nature
*Bible:* Genesis 1:31 (God saw everything he had made, and it was very good.)

## MATERIALS NEEDED

cord
orange juice lids, eight per child
½-pound plastic margarine tubs, one per child
stickers
paper punch
scissors
strapping tape

## GETTING READY
• Make a model to show the children.
• Cut four pieces of cord for each child and one piece for a hanger.

## HOW TO DO IT
• Let each child decorate eight lids with stickers.
• Punch eight holes around the edge of each tub and two in the bottom of the tub.
• Have children thread each piece of cord through two holes, leaving the ends hanging freely. Help children tape a cord end to each lid.
• Loop a cord through the holes in the bottom of the tub and tie the ends to make a hanger.

## VARIATIONS
• *For older children:* Tape eight-inch strips of crepe paper to the inside edge of the cup. Let the strips hang freely. Hang the cup following the directions above. Enjoy watching the wind blow the streamers.

## HOW DID IT GO?
• Could children identify places to hang their wind chime to make sounds in the wind?

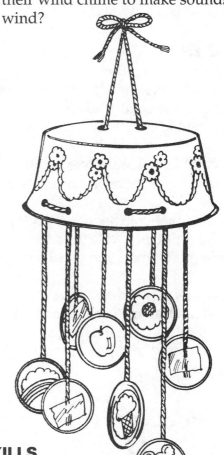

**SCIENCE DEVELOPMENT • THINKING SKILLS**

## MATERIALS NEEDED

wax paper
small glittery items such
   as sequins, flat beads,
   metallic wrapping paper
paper punch
iron
yarn
newspaper

# Window Hangings

*Children will discover how the sun helps create beauty.*

*Christian Values:* responding to God's world; enhancing self-esteem
*Bible:* Ecclesiastes 1:5 (The sun rises and the sun goes down.)

## GETTING READY

- For each child cut two 4- by 6-inch pieces of wax paper.
- Prepare your working space.

## HOW TO DO IT

- Talk about God's creation of the sun to give light. Observe the sunlight reflecting on the sequins to create beauty.
- Give each child two sheets of the wax paper.
- Ask the child to pick out several glittery items and arrange them on one sheet of wax paper.
- Put the other piece of wax paper on top. The teacher or helper will cover the wax paper with newspaper and press with a warm iron.
- When the wax paper sheets have stuck together, punch a hole in the top and tie a yarn hanger through it. Hang it at a window to catch the sun.

## VARIATIONS

- *For younger children:* Staple the edges instead of ironing the wax paper.
- *For older children:* Let the children cut their own wax paper sheets. With supervision, let them iron their window hangings.
- Cut a frame from the construction paper and mount the picture before hanging.

## HOW DID IT GO?

- What evidences of decision making and creative thinking did the children express?

# Make Crayons for Rubbings

*Children will turn something old into something new by recycling crayons.*

**Christian Values:** being good stewards; using God's gift of creativity
**Bible:** Genesis 1:27 (God made us with the ability to be creative.)

## MATERIALS NEEDED

old crayons
old muffin tin
vegetable oil or shortening
oven
wallpaper or other paper
  with raised pattern
leaf or coin
newsprint
masking tape

## GETTING READY
- Gather old crayons. Remove the paper.
- Preheat oven to 250 degrees.

## HOW TO DO IT
- Talk about recycling and caring for what we have.
- Grease the muffin tin.
- Break the crayons into the tin by color.
- Fill the tin with broken crayons. Heat until the crayons are melted.
- Remove the tin; let the crayons cool and harden. Remove the crayons.
- Place a leaf, a piece of paper with a raised pattern, or another flat object under a sheet of newsprint. Tape to the paper.
- Use the crayons to color over the raised area and see a pattern appear.

## VARIATIONS
- *For younger children:* Mix the colors in the tin for a multicolored effect.
- *For older children:* Provide adult supervision and let the children do all of the steps.

## HOW DID IT GO?
- Did the children understand and enjoy recycling art materials?
- What kinds of problem solving did you see as the children made rubbings?

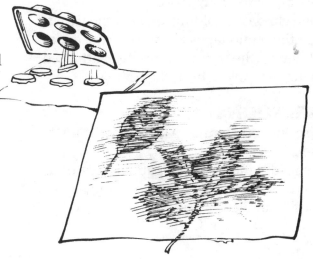

# Greeting Card Mobile

*Children will share a celebration with friends by making a mobile.*

*Christian Values:* making choices; developing a sense of community; responding to God
*Bible:* Psalm 75:1 (We give thanks to you, O God.)

## MATERIALS NEEDED

greeting cards showing children celebrating a specific holiday
shoebox (without lid)
yarn
cellophane tape
scissors
pencil

## GETTING READY

- Cut pieces of yarn about 20 inches long and one longer piece for a hanger. Make two holes in the bottom of the box. Thread the longer piece of yarn through them and tie the ends together to make the hanger.

## HOW TO DO IT

- Let each child choose a picture to cut out. Punch holes around the outer edge of the shoebox with a pencil. Thread each piece of yarn through two holes.
- One child can hold the ends of the yarn as another child tapes a picture to the ends. When all the pictures have been attached, hang the mobile from the ceiling.

## VARIATIONS

- Use colored snips of paper to decorate the box.
- Use old Sunday school papers or cards as sources of pictures to make a "Praise God" mobile.

- *For older children:* Take the box mobile to hang in a nursing home. Children may sing holiday songs or a happy birthday song to the residents.

## HOW DID IT GO?

- What symbols or customs did the children know?
- Did the children enjoy making the older people happy by their visit?

# Underwater Mobile

*Children will discover new wonders of God's world and create a mobile depicting life underwater.*

**Christian Values:** developing God's gift of creativity; awareness of God's world
**Bible:** Genesis 1:26 (People are to care for all life in God's world.)

## MATERIALS NEEDED

construction paper
 (assorted)
scissors
glue
markers
yarn
metal coat hanger
paper punch

## GETTING READY
- Cut construction paper into oval and triangle shapes.
- Cut smaller size rectangles for seaweed.
- Bend coat hangers to form circles.

## HOW TO DO IT
- Have children glue the oval and triangle together to make a fish.
- Fringe the edges of the rectangle to make seaweed.
- Color eyes and other details.
- Punch holes in top for hanging.
- Tie several pieces of yarn equally spaced around the hanger; then tie each piece of yarn to a mobile piece.

## VARIATIONS
- *For older children:* Children can cut their own shapes to make sea creatures.
- Use the hanger to create mobiles with other scenes such as animals or insects.

## HOW DID IT GO?
- Did the children use good thinking skills in creating the fish?

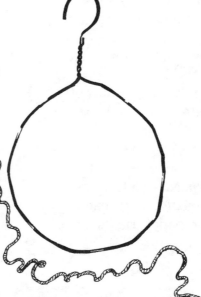
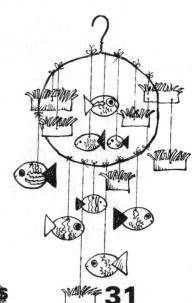

## MATERIALS NEEDED

12-inch dowels
felt or plain fabric
scissors
glue
yarn
magazines

# Feelings Banner

*Children will learn that feelings are all right and we can grow in responding positively to our feelings.*

*Christian Values:* appreciating God's love for us; growing in loving ways
*Bible:* Ephesians 4:15 (We are to grow up in every way.)

## GETTING READY
- Cut fabric into banners that are 8 by 12 inches.
- Cut out feelings pictures from magazines.

## HOW TO DO IT
- Give a banner and dowel to each child.
- Put feelings pictures on the table. Ask the children to choose pictures for their banners.
- Encourage children to talk about the feelings expressed in their pictures.
- Have the children glue the pictures onto the fabric. Write the title "Feelings Are OK" wherever the child wants it.
- Help the children glue one end of the fabric to the dowel. Add a yarn loop for hanging.

## VARIATIONS
- *For younger children:* Make a feelings book. Glue a feelings picture on each page of construction paper. Tie the pages together with a ribbon.

- *For older children:* Children can select their own pictures from the magazines and cut them out. Many can write the title by themselves.

## HOW DID IT GO?
- Do you see positive ways children handle their feelings?
- Are the children accepting of their feelings and how they express them?

# Berry Pretty Printing

*Children will learn the importance of recycling products by creating a pretty picture.*

*Christian Values:* caring for God's world; using our gift of creativity
*Bible:* Genesis 1:26 (People are to care for God's creation.)

## MATERIALS NEEDED

baskets for strawberries or blueberries
tempera paints
art paper
aluminum pie pans

## GETTING READY
• Mix tempera paints. Cover the bottom of the pie pans with a small amount of paint.
• Gather berry baskets and paper.

## HOW TO DO IT
• Dip the bottom of the berry basket into the paint.
• Press berry basket onto art paper several times.
• Repeat the process using different colors. Cover all the space on the paper.

## VARIATIONS
• Encourage children to discuss what they think their designs look like. They can add designs with crayon.
• Find other items that have different sizes and textures. Items need to be soft and absorbent to use for paint printing.
• Write on the back of the painting a feeling story that the child tells you about making the picture.

## HOW DID IT GO?
• What kinds of creative thinking did children use when painting?
• How can you display the paintings to make the art special and to help children feel proud of what they have done?

## MATERIALS NEEDED

bright colors of tempera
   paints
plastic drinking straws
water to thin paints
bowls for each color
art paper
dishwashing detergent

# Bubble Painting

*Children will use their creativity in painting a pretty design.*

**Christian Values:** developing self-esteem; developing God's gift of creativity
**Bible:** Genesis 1:27 (God gave us the gift of creativity.)

## GETTING READY
- Fill each bowl about one-third full of paint. Add a few drops of detergent.
- Thin the paint with a little water.
- Write each child's name on paper.
- Show children how to blow out with the straws rather than sucking in.

## HOW TO DO IT
- Blow into the paint through the straw until bubbles fill the bowl and begin to come over the top.
- If bubbles do not form, add a little more detergent or water.
- Lay a piece of paper over the bubbles. As they touch the paper, they will pop and leave a design of many circles.
- Continue using as many colors as desired, covering different areas of the paper.

## VARIATIONS
- *For younger children:* The blowing should be done by the teacher.
- *For older children:* After the paint dries on the paper, children can add crayon drawings.

## HOW DID IT GO?
- Did the children learn about taking turns in waiting for their turn to create?
- Were the children pleased with the effect the bubbles made on the paper?

# Corncob Printing

*Children will experience making a creative design using a recycled object.*

*Christian Values:* using God's gift of creativity; learning stewardship of earth's resources
*Bible:* Genesis 1:27 (God made us with the ability to be creative.)

## MATERIALS NEEDED

corncobs from frozen or
   fresh corn
tempera paints
paper towels
newsprint or construction
   paper
aluminum pie pans

## GETTING READY
- Dry corncobs in the sun.
- Place a few damp paper towels in a pie pan for each paint color.
- Have clean painting aprons.
- For washing hands, have a pan of water and paper towels ready.

## HOW TO DO IT
- Pour a small amount of thick paint on the damp paper towels in each pie pan. Place a cob in each container.
- Roll the corncob over the paint, making sure to cover the whole surface.
- Hold each end of the corncob. Roll the cob across the paper, printing in any direction.
- Use a variety of colors as desired. Less paint on the cob makes a prettier design.

## VARIATIONS
- Use small and large corncobs to vary the effect.
- Try making a print by stamping with the cob or using the end of the cob.

## HOW DID IT GO?
- Did the children enjoy the effect of the corncob on the paper?
- How do you know the children feel good about what they have created today?
- Was there evidence of awe, wonder, or good self-esteem? Say a thank-you prayer to God for "beautiful things I can do."

## MATERIALS NEEDED

tempera paint
firm sponges
large mural paper
patterns of animal
    footprints
aluminum pie plates
clothespins
books about animals

# Foot Fun

*Children will be able to compare the uniqueness of each animal print with their own footprint.*

*Christian Values:* recognizing the uniqueness of each part of God's creation; praising God
*Bible:* Genesis 1:25 (God made every kind of animal in the world.)

## GETTING READY
- Trace patterns of animal footprints onto sponge pieces and cut out.
- Put tempera paint in a pie plate or other shallow container.
- Clip a clothespin to the top of each sponge.

## HOW TO DO IT
- Have children dip the sponge pattern into the paint and press lightly onto the mural paper.
- Designs can be randomly spaced or in a pattern—as the children desire.
- Let children help wash and dry sponges thoroughly before they are stored.

## VARIATIONS
- Let children make their own footprints on long mural paper. Have children step into the pie plate of tempera paint and then step onto the mural.
- Write each child's name below the footprints. Have a basin of water and towels to wash and dry feet.

## HOW DID IT GO?
- What differences could the children point out in their feet and the animal footprints?
- Were the children willing to risk getting dirty? Were they willing to try something new?

# Gadget Painting

*Children will enjoy developing their creativity by painting with objects.*

*Christian Values:* using God's gift of creativity; enhancing self-esteem
*Bible:* Ephesians 4:15 (We are to grow up in every way.)

## MATERIALS NEEDED

kitchen gadgets such as:
  potato masher, egg
  whisk, cookie cutters
spools
paper towel rolls
tempera paint
meat tray, paper towels
newspaper
construction paper
paint smocks

## GETTING READY
- Cover the table with newspaper.
- Prepare paint pads by folding paper towels in a meat tray.
- Mix paint; pour over the paint pads.
- Gather all supplies.

## HOW TO DO IT
- Put out four or fewer pieces of paper.
- Place the paint pads and gadgets in the center of the table.
- Show the children how to press the gadget into the paint pad and then print on the paper.

## VARIATIONS
- Make more permanent paint pads by using a thin piece of foam in the meat tray. Let dry and use them again by adding a little water.

## HOW DID IT GO?
- Did the children take turns and share the materials?
- What evidence of creative thinking did you observe?

## MATERIALS NEEDED

crayons
white typing paper
1 tablespoon of blue
    powdered tempera
cup to mix paint
2 to 3 wide paintbrushes
books and pictures about
    spring
newspapers

# Spring With a Blue Wash

*Children will express their impressions of spring in a creative art activity.*

*Christian Values:* trusting in God; learning about God's plan for seasons; developing the gift of creativity

*Bible:* Genesis 8:22 (God plans for spring.)

## GETTING READY

• Cover painting area with newspaper.
• Mix 1 tablespoon blue paint with ⅔ cup water.

## HOW TO DO IT

• Discuss with the children the beauty of spring. Look at pictures and books about spring.
• Let children draw a sp___ ___ure. It is important that th__ ___ ___ ___ith the crayons an__ ___ ___ ___
• Then __ ___ ___ over ___ ___ will

## HOW DID IT GO?

• Did the children express wonder at the picture change with the blue wash?
• Did the art capture a feeling of spring?

*Spring time*
*Noah's Ark Story*
*"Rainbow Song"*
*pg. 168*

# Nipa Hut Mosaic

*Children will learn that people live in different kinds of homes and give thanks for God's care.*

**Christian Values:** appreciating and valuing others; praising God
**Bible:** Matthew 19:19 (Love your neighbor.)

## MATERIALS NEEDED

light cardboard cut into 8- by 11-inch sheets
copies of a nipa hut
glue
dried grass

## GETTING READY

- Display a picture of a nipa hut. Check your library or the mission study books for 1989–90.
- Make an outline drawing of a nipa hut. Photocopy patterns for each child.
- Make a sample of the nipa hut mosaic.

## HOW TO DO IT

- Talk about different kinds of homes the children live in. (Show the picture.) Say that most homes in the Philippines, especially in the country, are made of bamboo and palm leaves.
- Encourage children to talk about any experiences they have had with children from other countries or cultures.
- Give each child a sheet of cardboard and a copy of the nipa hut outline. Have the child glue the outline on the cardboard.
- Have the children glue dried grass on the roof and outside walls.

## VARIATIONS

- *For young children:* Children can tear bits of brown construction paper instead of grass and glue to the roof of the house. They can also color the walls and roof brown.
- *For older children:* Cut very narrow strips of brown construction paper and lay across the grass and roof. Staple at intervals to keep in place and make the house stronger.

## HOW DID IT GO?

- Did you sense any curiosity and appreciation of other people?
- Did children have any experiences with children of other cultures?

## MATERIALS NEEDED

strips of construction
   paper
safety scissors
glue
9-by-12 assorted
   construction paper
crayons
stapler

# Snip Art Mosaics

*Children will practice scissors skills and design an art project.*

*Christian Values:* enhancing self-esteem; developing God's gifts; celebrating growth
*Bible:* Genesis 1:27 (God made us with the ability to be creative.)

## GETTING READY
- Collect supplies needed.
- Write each child's name on a piece of construction paper.

## HOW TO DO IT
- Give each child several strips of construction paper or recycled scraps of paper.
- Show children how to hold the scissors and cut the paper into pieces by snipping.
- Let children put drops of glue on the 9-by-12 papers and arrange the snips in a free-style design.

## VARIATIONS
- *For younger children:* Draw a basic tree shape. Glue snips of fall colors to form leaves. In the spring use light green paper for leaves.
- *For older children:* Make a birthday crown by cutting a paper strip to fit the child's head. Staple ends together. Cut points on one edge to make a crown. Glue snipped pieces around the crown.

## HOW DID IT GO?
- Did the children feel good about their ability to use scissors successfully?
- Did you see thinking skills being used?

# Tissue Paper Butterfly

*Children will become aware of the beauty of God's world by creating beautiful butterflies.*

*Christian Values:* experiencing wonder at God's creation; expressing creativity
*Bible:* Ecclesiastes 3:11 (God has made everything beautiful.)

## MATERIALS NEEDED

construction paper (assorted)
typing paper
various colors of art tissue
scissors
white glue
small containers to mix glue
newspapers
pipe cleaners

## GETTING READY
- Cover work space with newspapers.
- Cut butterfly wings and body shapes out of construction paper.
- Mix 2 parts white glue with 1 part water.

## HOW TO DO IT
- Let children glue butterfly wings onto typing paper.
- Glue body shape to the center of the butterfly.
- Tear art tissue into small pieces. Arrange these on the white paper portion of the butterfly wings, overlapping colors to give a stained-glass effect.
- Apply glue mixture on top of the tissue using a brush.
- Add pipe cleaner antennas. Let dry.

## VARIATIONS
- *For younger children*: Decorate the wings by rolling small pieces of tissue into balls and gluing them on.
- *For older children*: Look at stage 4 of the Butterfly Cycle chart on page 186.

## HOW DID IT GO?
- Did the children enjoy watching the colors of the tissue blend?

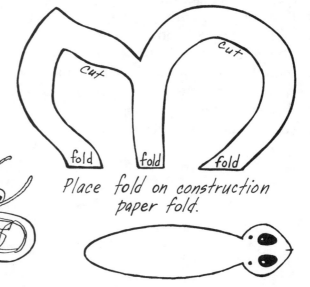

Place fold on construction paper fold.

## MATERIALS NEEDED

paper lunch bags
yarn
scraps of construction
   paper
scraps of fabric
markers
glue
newspaper
cardboard tubes
rubber bands

# Paper Bag Puppets

*Children will use their imagination to make puppets to use to tell stories.*

**Christian Values:** using God's gift of creativity; enhancing self-esteem
**Bible:** Genesis 1:26-28 (God made us with the ability to think and be creative.)

## GETTING READY
- Cover the table with newspaper.
- Put out the other materials in flat containers for children to use.
- Limit the number of children working at the table at one time.

## HOW TO DO IT
- Give each child a paper bag.
- Encourage children to select materials to create a puppet face on the bag.
- Stuff the puppets with newspaper.
- Hold the bag upside-down and put the cardboard tube into the bag to become the handle. Wrap yarn or a rubber band around the bottom of the puppet to hold the tube in place.
- Use the puppets to retell stories.

## VARIATIONS
- *For younger children:* Use flannelboard figures taped to craft sticks as puppets.
- *For older children:* Make puppets from craft sticks or socks. Make clothes from fabric scraps.

## HOW DID IT GO?
- In what ways were the children creative?
- Were they able to solve problems?

# Tube Sock Puppet

*Children will create a new way to express their thoughts and feelings.*

*Christian Values:* recognizing special talents of each person
*Bible:* Matthew 28:16-20 (Go to people everywhere and teach them.)

## MATERIALS NEEDED

one tube sock (child-size) per child
cardboard
felt-tip markers
glue
felt pieces

## GETTING READY
- Cut out the cardboard in the shape of a paddle or oar to fit inside the sock. Cut out two holes near the handle of the paddle.
- Cut the felt into circles and triangles.

## HOW TO DO IT
- Have each child put a paddle into a sock.
- Children will glue felt pieces to decorate their puppets with eyes, nose, hair, and clothing.
- Hold the puppet handle with one hand; put the thumb and forefinger through the holes from behind the puppet to make it talk. Hands stay outside the sock.

## VARIATIONS
- Draw around each child's foot and cut out the cardboard foot. Insert into sock.
- Let puppets tell how and where they could walk to follow Jesus.

## HOW DID IT GO?
- Could the children use the puppets to tell stories about Jesus?

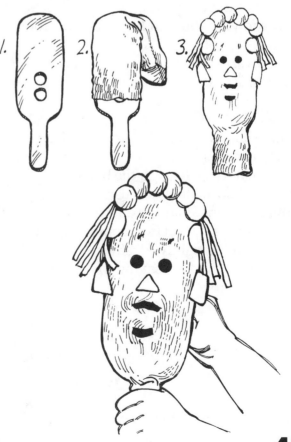

## MATERIALS NEEDED

large appliance or
  furniture box
yarn
wallpaper books
ribbon
other strip materials such
  as paper strips, fabric, or
  heavy yarn

# Weaving Box

*Children will respond creatively in a group experience.*

*Christian Values:* making choices; developing self-esteem; developing a sense of community
*Bible:* Genesis 1:26-28 (God made us with the ability to think and to learn.)

## GETTING READY

- Cut sections out of each box side. Punch holes in a line one inch away from top and bottom of opening.
- Thread yarn through holes to make four looms.
- Put a variety of weaving materials in trays for children to select.

## HOW TO DO IT

- Have box available during self-selected play time. Children may stand and weave any materials through the box loom.
- Show children how to push the yarn over and under and to alternate how each row is done. Use a comb to push the weaving tightly together.
- Add each child's weaving to a group project.

## VARIATIONS

- Cut and string individual box looms.

## HOW DID IT GO?

- Did children show appreciation for each other's contribution to the group project?

# Friendly Grahams

*Children will be able to work together and tell one way they can act in a friendly and kind way.*

*Christian Values:* showing kindness; respecting others

*Bible:* Proverbs 17:17 (A friend loves at all times.)

## MATERIALS NEEDED

graham crackers
vanilla icing and press
strips of paper 1 by 5
  inches

## GETTING READY

- Print questions on strips of paper that start, "What could a friend do if . . . " (for example: "someone were hungry?")
- Make a sample. Using two graham squares, squeeze icing near the edge of one. Fold a question and place it in the middle of the cracker. Cover the paper and the icing with a second cracker.

## HOW TO DO IT

- Use Friendly Grahams to stimulate conversation about kind behaviors.
- Let each child make a Friendly Graham sandwich. Place each child's sandwich on a napkin with his or her name on it.
- At snack time, read each question. Encourage each child to give an appropriate answer.

## VARIATIONS

- *For younger children:* Place a picture of a situation to identify and respond to inside each cracker sandwich.

## HOW DID IT GO?

- Which questions encouraged the most enthusiasm from the children? Were their answers appropriate?
- Were there any questions that the children appeared to not understand?

## MATERIALS NEEDED

bread slices
any fruit jelly
shallow plates
alphabet cereal
plastic knives

# Name Sandwiches

*Children will form their names as they make their snacks.*

**Christian Values:** thanking God for developing
skills; enhancing self-esteem
**Bible:** Psalm 92:1 (It is good to thank God.)

## GETTING READY
• Have children wash their hands before
doing this activity.

## HOW TO DO IT
• Put alphabet cereal and jelly on shallow
plates for each two children at the tables.
• Give each child a bread slice. Ask
children to spread fruit jelly on the slices.
• Tell children to select the appropriate
letters and arrange them on the bread to
write their names.

## VARIATIONS
• *For young children:* Have children pick
out any letter and tell you its name before
they put it on the bread.
• The teacher can pick out the letters of
their names and help them name them.

## HOW DID IT GO?
• How many more of your children need
help in recognizing and writing their
names?
• Could they use the knife to spread their
own jelly?

# Easy Fudge

## MATERIALS NEEDED

ingredients for fudge
heating element
clear glass double boiler
spoon or spatula
square cake pan
table knife

*Children will enjoy working together to make fudge for Christmas.*

**Christian Values:** sharing and taking turns; working together; giving to others

**Bible:** Romans 12:4-7 (God has given us different gifts that can be used to help people.)

## GETTING READY
- Assemble the ingredients and equipment on a low table where children can work.
- Print the recipe with pictures on a chart.

## HOW TO DO IT
- Follow the recipe. Children can take turns "reading" the recipe chart, measuring, and adding the ingredients to the top of the double boiler.
- Mix and cook over hot water until smooth. Stir infrequently.

## VARIATIONS
- Let each child put a few pieces in a zipper bag to share with family or friends.
- Use as a gift for someone special.
- *For older children:* Use as a cooking activity to teach the letter *F*.

## HOW DID IT GO?
- Did the children patiently take turns?
- Which children were afraid to risk? How will you help them?

Easy Fudge

16-ounce box of powdered sugar
½ cup cocoa
¼ teaspoon salt
6 tablespoons margarine
4 tablespoons milk
1 tablespoon vanilla
1 cup nuts

Powdered Sugar XXXXXX

Margarine

MILK

Mix all ingredients, except nuts, in the double boiler. Cook over boiling water until smooth. Add nuts and mix together. Pour into square cake pan. Cool. Cut into squares.

# Doughnuts

## MATERIALS NEEDED

refrigerator biscuits
cooking oil
electric frying pan or small
   deep fry
wax paper
powdered sugar
small lunch bag
paper towels

*Children will prepare doughnuts and enjoy eating them together.*

**Christian Values:** enhancing self-esteem; sharing; cooperating
**Bible:** Acts 2:46 (Early Christians ate together.)

## GETTING READY

- Ask a parent or aide to help with this activity.
- For safety reasons one adult needs to handle the frying.
- Set up cooking space so children can safely observe the frying.
- Pour oil in skillet and heat.

## HOW TO DO IT

- Let children make a medium-size hole in the middle of each biscuit.
- An adult drops the doughnut shape into the oil. If you use a frying pan, turn the doughnuts.
- When the doughnuts are golden brown, cool them briefly on paper towels.
- Make sugar doughnuts by shaking the doughnuts in a lunch bag with powdered sugar.
- Best eaten warm. Delicious!

## VARIATIONS

- *For younger children:* Shake doughnuts in cinnamon and sugar.
- *For older children:* Use doughnuts to emphasize the letter *D*.

## HOW DID IT GO?

- Were the children eager to share their doughnuts?
- Were children able to observe the safety precautions?

# The Apple Tree

### MATERIALS NEEDED

two or three apples
knife
sequence pictures of the
    growth of an apple seed
rhyme "The Apple"
paper towels or napkins

*Children will discover that God plans for an apple tree to grow from a seed.*

**Christian Values:** discovering God's plan for growth; discovering God's world

**Bible:** Genesis 1:11-12 (God created plants with seeds that will grow.)

## GETTING READY
• Learn the brief rhyme.

## HOW TO DO IT
• Cut an apple crosswise and show the children the star formation of the seeds. Talk about how a big apple tree grew out of seeds like these.
• Say a prayer of thanksgiving for God's plan for the apple tree.
• Teach this rhyme:

> **The Apple**
> Look at this apple.
> It came from a tree.
> Cut it up, and what do you see?
> Tiny brown seeds,
> To grow into an apple tree .

## VARIATIONS
• Have an adult remove the core from several apples and slice the apples crosswise.
• Let the children spread peanut butter on each slice for a snack.

• *For older children:* Ask the children to arrange the pictures in sequence and tell the story of an apple seed or say the rhyme.
• Save some seeds to plant later.

## HOW DID IT GO?
• Did the children express wonder at the star formation?
• How did the children respond to the rhyme?

## MATERIALS NEEDED

bananas
shallow bowl of honey
plate of wheat germ
toothpicks
napkins
table knife
serving plate

# Banana Bites

*Children will prepare a snack and share it with the class.*

*Christian Values:* enhancing self-esteem; sharing; caring for body

*Bible:* Acts 2:46 (Early Christians worshiped and ate together in their homes.)

### GETTING READY

- Place the ingredients on a table.
- Show the children how to make the banana bites.

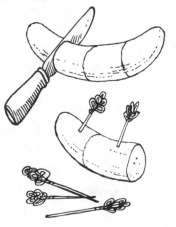

### HOW TO DO IT

- Emphasize safety precautions in using the knife and toothpicks.
- Talk about foods to eat to keep a healthy body. Check food allergies.
- Peel the bananas; cut into four pieces.
- Insert a toothpick in each.
- Dip in honey; roll in wheat germ.
- Enjoy eating at snacktime.

### VARIATIONS

- Use apples and let the children cut them with an apple cutter.

### HOW DID IT GO?

- How can you build community by eating together?

# Fruit Basket

*Children will grow in appreciation of God's world of nature by naming different fruits.*

**Christian Values:** appreciating God's plan for food; praising God's care
**Bible:** Psalm 92:1 (It is good to give thanks to God.)

## MATERIALS NEEDED

four identical sets of six fruit stickers
cube made from light cardboard
three-by-five cards
glue
basket or container

## GETTING READY
- Make a picture cube according to the diagram. Use one set of stickers to glue a picture on each side of the cube.
- Mount the other three sets on three-by-five cards (one picture to a card).

## HOW TO DO IT
- Give each player (three players at most) six different cards and ask them to name the fruits.
- Children take turns throwing the cube on the floor or table and matching the picture on the top of the cube with one of their cards. Put the card in the basket.
- Continue playing the game until all the children have put their cards in the fruit basket.
- Say a prayer to thank God for many kinds of good fruit.

## VARIATIONS
- *For young children:* Let a child pick out a card and name the fruit.
- Spread the cards on the table, pick one up, and ask: "John, can you find a picture that looks like this?"

## HOW DID IT GO?
- Were the children able to follow the rules and play the game?
- Which foods did the children indicate they liked the best?

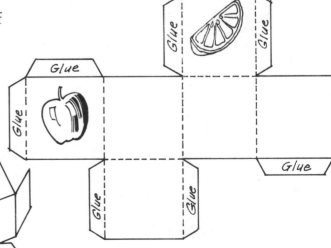

**SCIENCE DEVELOPMENT • THINKING SKILLS**

# Fruit Salad Bar

## MATERIALS NEEDED

fruit salad ingredients:
  canned peach slices,
  canned pear slices,
  bananas, whipped
  topping, graham
  crackers
plastic knife and cutting
  board
rolling pin and plastic bag
bowls and spoons

*Children will learn to follow a sequence of directions by making a salad.*

**Christian Values:** completing a task; enhancing self-esteem; caring for one's body
**Bible:** Genesis 1:27 (We were created by God and are to care for our bodies.)

## GETTING READY

- Prepare a recipe poster for the salad using pictures and labels from cans or boxes.
- Invite an extra adult to assist.
- Check for children who have food allergies.
- Line up bowls of ingredients in the same order as they appear on the poster.

## HOW TO DO IT

- Let children crush graham crackers and cut the fruit in slices or small chunks.
- Let children read the poster and mix their own salad in the sequence given.

## VARIATIONS

- If fresh fruits are in season, let older children wash and cut a variety of fresh fruits for salad. Teacher may prepeel or precut fruits that children can chop.
- Make a tossed vegetable salad. Younger children can tear lettuce. Older children can clean and cut celery or peppers and grate carrots and cheese.

## HOW DID IT GO?

- How did children respond to the opportunity for independence?

# Sugarless Applesauce

*Children will prepare food and share with the class or family members.*

*Christian Values:* enhancing self-esteem; sharing with others

*Bible:* Acts 2:46 (Members of the Christian community share their food and eat together.)

## MATERIALS NEEDED

six or more tart apples
⅓ cup apple juice
   concentrate
½ cup water
large spoon
cutting board
plastic picnic knives
electric skillet
paper cups
small spoon for each child

## GETTING READY
- Talk with the children about safety and show how to use the knife and skillet.

## HOW TO DO IT
- Let the children wash the apples and take turns cutting unpeeled apples.
- Put the chopped apples into the skillet.
- Let older children help measure and pour the apple juice and water into the skillet.
- Cook the apples on low heat for about twenty minutes.
- Cool; spoon into cups.
- Enjoy eating with the class.

## VARIATIONS
- *For younger children:* Put the prepared applesauce into small recycled plastic containers for each child to take home and share with the family.
- *For older children:* Put the prepared applesauce into a recycled plastic container to be shared with another class.
- Encourage children to think of persons or agencies who might like to have some applesauce and give some to them.

## HOW DID IT GO?
- Were the children able to use the plastic knives safely?
- Did the children express appreciation to God and to each other for the applesauce?

## MATERIALS NEEDED

instant banana pudding
milk
small, sterilized baby food
jars
tablespoon measuring
spoon
small bowls and plastic
spoons

# Shake a Pudding

*Children will learn one of God's laws of nature as they discover changes when making some pudding.*

**Christian Values:** discovering God's wonderful works; responding to God in praise
**Bible:** Psalm 105:1, 2 (We are thankful for all of the wonders of God's world.)

## GETTING READY

- Show children the powdered form of the pudding and the liquid form of the milk. What happens when they are mixed together?
- Tell children that when the powder is put together with the milk, a change will appear.

## HOW TO DO IT

- Let children measure 1 tablespoon of pudding mix and 2 tablespoons of milk and pour into a jar.
- With lid tightly on, allow a child to shake the jar until the powder and milk form pudding.
- Spoon pudding into small bowls or paper cups.

## VARIATIONS

- The total quantity of the pudding and milk may be mixed in a large jar or plastic container. (See package directions.)

## HOW DID IT GO?

- Were there any problems with the children and their measuring?
- Can they retell the story of making the pudding?
- Were the children able to count and to measure the food correctly?

# Crispy Cheese Animals

*Children will take turns and share as they prepare their snack.*

*Christian Values:* sharing with others; respecting others' rights
*Bible:* Acts 2:46 (God's children share with one another)

## MATERIALS NEEDED

soft tortillas (one package of ten yields about twenty-four animals)
animal-shaped cookie cutters
bacon bits
grated cheddar cheese
cookie tray

## GETTING READY
- Arrange for extra adult help.
- Grate the cheddar cheese.
- Make plans with another class for sharing the snacks.

## HOW TO DO IT
- Let the children use cookie cutters to cut animal shapes out of the tortillas.
- Place them on a cookie tray.
- Spread grated cheese and bacon bits on top.
- Explain safety rules about working in the kitchen and using the oven.
- Have an adult put the cookie sheet under the broiler for three to five minutes. Children may help you set the timer.
- Cool the cheese before serving.
- Share with another class.

## VARIATIONS
- *For young children:* Use bread slices instead of tortillas.
- Share snacks with members of the staff.

## HOW DID IT GO?
- How did you organize your time so that the children did not have to wait too long for their turns?
- Did everyone participate in the activity? How did you encourage those who were hesitant?

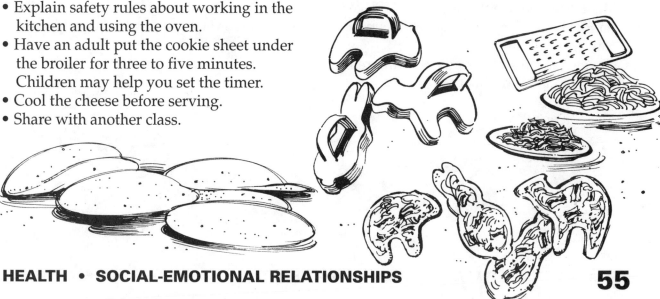

# Math Trail Mix

## MATERIALS NEEDED

two or three varieties of
  cereal
raisins
peanuts
bowls for ingredients
large bowl for mixing
plain paper towels
marker

*Children will practice health and math skills as they prepare a snack to eat.*

*Christian Values:* enhancing self-esteem; developing thinking skills and math readiness
*Bible:* Genesis 1:26 (God has given us minds to think with.)

## GETTING READY
- Place all ingredients in small bowls and mix together.
- For each child use a marker to divide a paper towel into four or five vertical columns.
- Have children wash their hands.

## HOW TO DO IT
- Discuss each ingredient. Have children tell how they are alike and different (size, shape, texture).
- Mix ingredients in the large bowl. Place a handful of trail mix on each child's paper towel.
- Have children sort the mix into different rows by classification.

## VARIATIONS
- *For older children:* Have children sort the food as you give directions: Put four raisins in a row; put three round pieces of cereal in a row, and so on.
- Ask: "Which row has the most?" "Which has the least?" "Can you make all the rows even by eating pieces in certain rows?"
- Let children put remainder of mix into the bowl and enjoy the snack.

## HOW DID IT GO?
- Were children thinking mathematically?
- What words were new to the children?

**MATH READINESS • HEALTH • LANGUAGE DEVELOPMENT**

# Mini Pizzas

**MATERIALS NEEDED**

English muffins
spaghetti sauce
mozzarella cheese
pepperoni (optional)
small toaster oven
napkins and paper plates

*Children will enjoy sharing in preparation of and eating a different snack.*

**Christian Values:** eating together in Christian fellowship; working together
**Bible:** Acts 2:46 (Members of the Christian community shared their food.)

## GETTING READY
- Place materials on a large table.
- Prepare to tell the Bible story from Acts.
- Grate the cheese. (If children are old enough, let them do this.)
- Slice the muffins in half.

## HOW TO DO IT
- Talk with the children about how nice it is to share a meal with friends. Then tell the Bible story from Acts.
- Give each child one-half of an English muffin.
- Have children spread about one tablespoonful of spaghetti sauce on the muffin slice.
- Have the children add grated cheese, pepperoni, and other toppings.
- Place a few muffins in the oven just long enough to melt the cheese.

## VARIATIONS
- *For older children:* Arrange the ingredients in stations. Encourage cooperation by allowing one group of children to spread the sauce, then the next group add cheese, and so on. Call it a "cooperative pizza."

## HOW DID IT GO?
- Were the children cooperative in doing the activity? Could they wait their turns?
- Can they recall the steps used in preparing the pizza?

# Make Peanut Butter

**MATERIALS NEEDED**

blender
1 cup peanuts
1 tablespoon peanut oil
crackers
table knife
measuring cup
tablespoon

*Children will make peanut butter from peanuts.*

*Christian Values:* enhancing self-esteem; sharing with friends
*Bible:* Genesis 1:29 (God has given us plants for food.)

## GETTING READY
- Assemble ingredients on a low table.
- Plan other activities children can do while you work in the small group.
- Gather as many ways to use peanuts as possible. Be very cautious using nuts with young children.

## HOW TO DO IT
- Seat a small group of children so each child can see the blender.
- Pour peanuts into blender.
- Add oil.
- Blend until fairly smooth.
- Spread on crackers.

## VARIATIONS
- *For younger children:* Introduce the word *peanuts*. Let children touch and smell the shells, and taste the nuts. Let the teacher break open the shells and see the nuts inside.
- *For older children:* Use peanuts to teach the letter *P*.
- Use pictures or books to show children how peanuts grow underground.
- Have a peanut day. Enjoy learning as much as you can about peanuts. Eat peanuts in as many ways as you can: roasted, boiled, peanut brittle, cookies, honey peanuts, and so on.

## HOW DID IT GO?
- What was the children's reaction as they watched the peanuts change form?

# Farmer's Haystacks

*Children will learn to work together as they prepare a snack to share for a celebration.*

**Christian Values:** being thankful for food; reaching out to others
**Bible:** Genesis 1:29 (God gives us many things to have for food.)

## MATERIALS NEEDED

For two dozen haystacks:
one 6-ounce package of butterscotch chips
one 6-ounce package of chocolate chips
one 3-ounce can Chinese noodles
double boiler and hot plate
stirring spoon
can opener

## GETTING READY
- Cut and mount pictures of farms with haystacks.

## HOW TO DO IT
- Show pictures of the haystacks and talk about them with the children. What are they made of? What shape are they and why? What does the farmer do with them?
- Show ingredients to the children and say that they will make some candy haystacks.
- With children a safe distance away, melt both kinds of chips in a double boiler on low heat.
- Add noodles and mix well.
- Drop by tablespoonfuls onto wax paper and let cool.
- Say a prayer of thanksgiving for the many foods that God has given us.

## VARIATIONS
- Use this activity during the fall season, as a Halloween activity, to share with another class, or to eat as a special treat to celebrate a birthday.
- *For older children:* Talk about what happened to the chips when they were heated. What happened when they cooled?

## HOW DID IT GO?
- Did the children enjoy the combination of tastes and texture of this treat?
- Did they assume responsibility for taking turns, sharing, and cleaning up afterwards?

**SCIENCE DEVELOPMENT • SOCIAL-EMOTIONAL RELATIONSHIPS**

## MATERIALS NEEDED

potatoes, onions, celery
canned tomatoes, carrots,
  mixed vegetables
beef broth cubes
package of noodles
Crockpot
large stirring spoon,
  plastic knives, mixing
  bowls, vegetable brush,
  can opener
pan of water

# Friendship Soup

*Children will recognize the importance of sharing what we have with others.*

*Christian Values:* sharing what we have; working cooperatively
*Bible:* Matthew 14:17-21 (Jesus used a little food to share with many people.)

## GETTING READY
• Send home an assigned list of food that each child will bring. Plan extra in case someone forgets.

## HOW TO DO IT
• Let each child show the food he or she brought. Ask each one: "Is this enough for all of us?"
• Tell children: "If we all share the food and cook it together, there will be enough for all."
• Let children chop and prepare vegetables for the soup. Teachers should open the cans of food.
• Allow each child to take turns adding food to the soup in a cool Crockpot.
• Turn the Crockpot on and allow soup to cook following directions.

## VARIATIONS
• Read or tell the story *Stone Soup.*
• Serve the food for snacks. Talk about what happens when everyone shares.

## HOW DID IT GO?
• Did the children easily share their food?
• Can they name the foods needed to make soup?

# One Potato, Two Potatoes

Children will recognize God's plan for food to eat, and begin to recognize numerals as they play the game.

**Christian Values:** appreciating God's plan for food; learning to use the ability to think
**Bible:** Genesis 2:9 (God made the trees that grow food.)

## MATERIALS NEEDED

brown construction paper
markers
scissors

## GETTING READY
- Cut out potatoes from construction paper large enough for the children to stand on. Write the numbers 1 to 10 on them.
- Cut out and label five smaller potatoes, but large enough for the children to stand on.

## HOW TO DO IT
- Count the potatoes with the children.
- Learn and recite this rhyme:
    One potato, two potatoes
    Three potatoes, four
    Five potatoes, six potatoes,
    Seven potatoes, more
    Eight potatoes, nine potatoes
    Here is ten.
- Lay the "potatoes" on the floor and let each child take turns jumping on the correct potato as the number is called.

## VARIATIONS
- *For younger children:* Show the younger children the *little* and *big* potatoes. Spread them on the floor and ask five children at a time to step on the appropriate potato as the size is called.
- *For older children:* Talk about potatoes. Talk about their color, taste, food group, whether they grow above or below the ground.

## HOW DID IT GO?
- Could the children share and take turns?
- Was this game a good way to review their numbers?

**LARGE-MUSCLE SKILLS • MATH READINESS**

## MATERIALS NEEDED

recipe for rice salad
cooking bowls
utensils
chart paper
marking pen
measuring cups
measuring spoons
individual bowls and
   plastic spoons
plastic serrated knives

# Rice Salad

*Children will work together in preparing a special treat for others.*

*Christian Values:* enhancing independence and self-esteem; sharing with others
*Bible:* Ephesians 4:15 (We are to grow in every way.)

## GETTING READY

- Prepare the recipe chart using symbols for the amounts, and labels or illustrations for the ingredients.
- Display at the child's eye level near the food preparation area.

## HOW TO DO IT

- Let children follow the recipe chart to make individual salads.

### Rice Salad (per child)

Mix: ½ cup chilled cooked rice
   ¼ cup pineapple tidbits
   2 tablespoons minimarshmallows
   1 tablespoon chopped cherries
   3 tablespoons whipped topping

## VARIATIONS

- *For older children:* Let children work together to make a group salad instead of individual salads.
- Invite another class to visit and enjoy the snack you made.

## HOW DID IT GO?

- Were children able to make the snack? Was it accepted better than an adult-prepared snack?

# Butter Shake

Children will discover one of the wonders of God's world by watching cream turn into butter.

**Christian Values:** learning Bible background; appreciating wonders in God's world
**Bible:** Proverbs 30:33 (The churning of milk produces butter.)

## MATERIALS NEEDED

small sterilized jars
heavy cream
salt
pinch of sugar

## GETTING READY
• Assemble all materials.

## HOW TO DO IT
• Ask children to tell how they get butter in today's world.
• Tell a story about how butter was made long ago in Bible times.
• Tell children that they will have a chance to make butter.
• Pour heavy cream into a jar about one-half full. Add salt and a pinch of sugar.
• Have children take turns shaking the jar. Keep shaking until the cream turns to butter. (It will separate and solidify into butter and water.)
• Drain the water. Mold the butter and rinse with clear water.
• Spread butter on crackers or bread.

## VARIATIONS
• *For younger children:* Adults may shake the jar of butter and let the children watch. They may want to help momentarily, but their attention span is too short.
• Butter may be placed in a small gelatin mold, refrigerated, and unmolded to make it look pretty.

## HOW DID IT GO?
• Do you think the children appreciate how hard people had to work long ago to make butter?

**SCIENCE DEVELOPMENT • SOCIAL-EMOTIONAL RELATIONSHIPS**

# Can Eat—Can't Eat

## MATERIALS NEEDED

three or four pieces of tagboard
three or four drapery rings (or cardboard rings)
glue
scissors
pictures of foods and household poisons

*Children will learn the difference between edible food and nonedible substances.*

*Christian Values:* learning God's plan for food; caring for our bodies
*Bible:* Genesis 1:29 (God provides the food our bodies need.)

## GETTING READY

- Make food charts: glue pictures of food as well as pictures of poisonous substances used in the home (bleach, cleaning fluid, medicine, and so on) on the tagboard.

## HOW TO DO IT

- Play this game individually.
- Lay a chart flat on the floor. Ask the child to put a ring on the category you ask for, such as "Put a ring on something you can eat" or "something you can't eat."
- Ask the child to name the food or item he or she puts a ring on.

## VARIATIONS

- Paste pictures of food and poisonous substances on cards to hold up.
- On the bottom of a shallow box glue a happy face and an angry face. Ask the child to put the food card on the happy face and the poisonous item on the angry face.

## HOW DID IT GO?

- Could the children identify and name the poisonous substances?
- Were they able to make the right choices as you played the game?

**HEALTH • THINKING SKILLS**

# Feed Dorothy

### MATERIALS NEEDED

a grocery bag
small basket
magazines
scissors
markers
glue
scraps of felt
yarn

*Children will grow in how to care for their bodies by learning to eat the proper foods.*

*Christian Values:* appreciating God's gifts; caring for our bodies; developing our minds
*Bible:* Genesis 1:29-31 (God has given us food, and it is good.)

## GETTING READY

- Create a face of "Dorothy" (a child) on one side of a grocery bag. Cut out the mouth big enough for food pictures to go in. Decorate with yarn and felt pieces. Stand bag upright.
- Cut out pictures of food from the basic food groups and place in a small basket.

## HOW TO DO IT

- Put "Dorothy" and the basket in the middle of the children.
- Say: "It's time for Dorothy's dinner. We'll feed her nutritious food." Each child picks a food from the basket, names it, and tells the food group to which it belongs. Then the food is fed through Dorothy's mouth until all foods are used.

## VARIATIONS

- *For younger children:* Have the children name the food that they fed Dorothy.
- *For older children:* Have pictures of nutritious foods and junk foods. Let children practice making choices of which food is good to eat.

## HOW DID IT GO?

- Do your children need more help in choosing good foods to eat?
- Is there carryover between the game and what the children choose to eat?
- Are there children in your class who do not receive nutritious meals? What will you do?

# Picnic Play

## MATERIALS NEEDED

picnic basket
blanket
snack foods
cups and juice
napkins
plastic knives
more adult helpers

*Children will identify a new way to enjoy time together with friends and to celebrate nature.*

*Christian Values:* respecting creation; developing a sense of community
*Bible:* Acts 17:24 (God made the world and everything in it.)

## GETTING READY
- Locate a basket to use. Buy any supplies needed for food preparation.
- Take a walk to discover God's gifts that you can point out to the children.

## HOW TO DO IT
- Let the children help prepare a simple, nutritious snack and pack it in the picnic basket. Use foods such as peanut butter and crackers, cheese bits, fruit chunks, juices, and nuts.
- Walk around the yard or to a nearby park. Encourage children to point out gifts God has created for us to use.
- Spread out the blanket and encourage children to sit close together. Say a grace by naming some of God's gifts.

## VARIATIONS
- *For older children:* Children can plan and make their own picnic lunch of finger foods.
- Let children pack the foods in individual egg cartons. Use foods such as raisins and nuts, carrot sticks, egg slices, and cheese cubes with crackers.
- See food activities on pages 50, 55, 56, and 65.

## HOW DID IT GO?
- Were children able to thank God more easily for gifts of creation after the walk?
- Did the children remember which foods promote good health?

# Taste Treat

*Children will learn about God's care for people in other cultures by tasting foods from various cultures.*

*Christian Values:* valuing uniqueness in each person; realizing God's care for all
*Bible:* Ephesians 2:19 (We are all members of the family of God.)

## MATERIALS NEEDED

foods from a variety of cultures: burritos, tropical fruits, peanut soup
pictures of children from these cultures
plastic serrated knives
paper plates
festive napkins
music from countries represented, if desired

## GETTING READY
- Check for food allergies in class.
- Identify foods, traditions, and music in a variety of cultures or countries.

## HOW TO DO IT
- Let children help with the preparation of the foods when possible.
- Talk about parts of the foods that may be familiar to your children—lettuce or tomatoes in tacos, peanuts in the soup.
- Play the music and use the napkins to create a festive atmosphere as children explore tastes, smells, textures, and appearance of the new foods.
- Talk about God's plan for food for all people wherever they live. Say a prayer of thanks for new foods to enjoy.

## VARIATIONS
- Include foods familiar to different areas of the United States such as grits, corn pudding, or wild rice.
- Invite someone who can share more of the culture with the children—clothing, celebrations, music, language.

## HOW DID IT GO?
- What characteristics of the foods made them most acceptable to the children?
- Which children were afraid to try new tastes? How can you work with the family to overcome this fear?

# Tidbit Tasting

## MATERIALS NEEDED

 napkins
small plates
variety of fresh fruit
water
cups
serrated plastic knives

*Children will explore various foods through using their senses.*

**Christian Values:** learning through the senses; experiencing wonder and awe
**Bible:** Genesis 1:29 (God has provided all kinds of grains and fruit to eat.)

## GETTING READY
- Be aware of food allergies of children.
- Clean, cut, arrange foods for tasting.

## HOW TO DO IT
- Talk about some foods that your children like. Point out that different people like different foods.
- Use different senses to become acquainted with the food (smell, taste, feel).
- Encourage children to taste at least one new food and discuss the similarities and differences with familiar foods.
- Sing or say a prayer of thanks to God for good foods to eat.

## VARIATIONS
- *For older children:* Make the tasting party an adventure by trying raw vegetables, pasta, and so on.
- Provide cutting boards, knives, and washing area for children to take turns preparing for the tasting party. Supervise very carefully.

## HOW DID IT GO?
- What foods were best accepted?
- Did familiarity with foods help the children's willingness to taste the food?
- Were there foods the children did not like? How can you prepare them differently another time?

# Ball and Box Roll

*Children will develop their large-muscle skills and learn to work together.*

*Christian Values:* developing self-discipline; understanding interdependence of people
*Bible:* Proverbs 20:11 (Even children are known by their acts.)

## MATERIALS NEEDED

long narrow boxes
sponge balls

## GETTING READY
- Cut the sides of the boxes to three inches high.

## HOW TO DO IT
- Group pairs of children on the floor so that they are facing each other.
- Give each pair a box and a ball.
- Show the children how to raise and lower the ends of the box (like a seesaw) to cause the ball to roll.
- Children work together to keep the ball from rolling out of the box. If it rolls out, change partners and begin the game again. Avoid competition.

## VARIATIONS
- For a group to play outside, use beach balls and a large beach towel or a sheet. Children can stand and hold the sheet around the edges. The object is to work together to keep the ball from hitting the ground.

## HOW DID IT GO?
- Did the cooperative experience seem too stressful for any of the children?

## MATERIALS NEEDED

- drinking straws
- cotton balls
- crayons
- toothpicks
- paper clips
- pieces of chalk
- other small items
- chart paper
- marking pen

# Blowing Game

*Children will discover God's laws of creation by classifying objects that are easy or hard to move by blowing.*

**Christian Values:** appreciating God's gift of the ability to think; understanding creation
**Bible:** Proverbs 2:6 (God gives understanding.)

## GETTING READY

- Demonstrate how to blow through the straw to move an object. Show children how to classify each object based on their experience in blowing.
- This game is played individually.

## HOW TO DO IT

- Place several small items of varying sizes, weight, or shapes on the table. Draw a *Begin* and an *End* line on the table with chalk.
- Have a child blow each object toward the finish line. Limit the number of times a child can blow at an object.
- Make a chart with three columns that say: (1) Easy to move, (2) Hard to move, and (3) Could not move at all. After the child blows the object, have the child place each object under the appropriate heading.

## VARIATIONS

- Fill a plastic tub three-quarters full of water. Place one or two table-tennis balls in the tub. Children will blow the balls from one side of the tub to the other.
- Talk about why some things moved easier than others did.

## HOW DID IT GO?

- Which children need more work in classifying?
- Did any of the children want to play the game again?

# Musical Carpet Squares

*Children will learn to cooperate with others by playing a musical game.*

*Christian Values:* valuing others; using God's
  gifts cooperatively
*Bible:* Ephesians 4:32 (Be kind to one another.)

## MATERIALS NEEDED

record player or cassette
music
carpet squares (one per
  child)

## GETTING READY
- Use nonskid carpet squares.
- Put ten carpet squares in a circle. If there are more than ten children, make more circles.

## HOW TO DO IT
- When music starts, ten children walk around the circle. Stop the music. Children must stop on a carpet square.
- Remove a carpet square and repeat the process. When music stops, everyone must stand on a square (so two must share one of the squares).
- Play again. Each time the music stops, remove another square. Children must share with those who have no square.
- Continue until all children are sharing one square: all must be able to touch the square with some part of the foot.

## VARIATIONS
- *For younger children:* Let younger children walk from one square to another until the music stops. When children stop on the carpets, let them jump, sway, stretch, and so on. Repeat game.

## HOW DID IT GO?
- Did the group show that they enjoyed solving a problem so all could succeed?

# Push-Croquet

## MATERIALS NEEDED

large beach balls or
   playground balls
sturdy cardboard boxes
   several inches taller than
   the balls
masking tape
sharp knife (for the
   teacher)

*Children will play a game to sharpen eye–hand coordination and to cooperate with classmates.*

**Christian Values:** enhancing self-esteem;
   valuing other children
**Bible:** Galatians 5:13 (Serve one another in
   love.)

## GETTING READY

- Cut arches in opposite sides of each box so that the balls can easily roll through.
- Place boxes three to five feet apart on the floor.
- Use masking tape to form a trail between the boxes.

## HOW TO DO IT

- Let children crawl on their knees or bend from the waist to push a ball along the taped trail and through the box arches.
- As children wait for their turn, let them sit around the course and roll the ball back to a player when the ball leaves the game area.

## VARIATIONS

- *For younger children:* Let two-year-olds sit opposite each other in pairs. Place a box between them. Encourage them to roll the ball back and forth to each other through the box arch.
- *For older children:* Have children sit or stand at a designated spot about a foot from the box and try to roll the ball through the arches.

## HOW DID IT GO?

- Did the game setup allow for enough space so that conflict was avoided?

# Find the Clock

## MATERIALS NEEDED

a clock that makes a sound

*Children will locate the clock by listening to its sound.*

*Christian Values:* developing God's gift of hearing; praising God
*Bible:* Genesis 1:26-28 (God made us with the ability to learn through our senses.)

## GETTING READY
• Talk about what it would be like if the children could not hear.

## HOW TO DO IT
• Show the children the clock. Listen to its sound.
• Ask the children to close their eyes while you hide it. Select one child each time to find it by listening for it. The child who finds it may hide it the next time.
• Choose another child to be "It" and continue the game. Play as long as the interest is high or until all who want to have had a chance to hide and find the clock.

## VARIATIONS
• *For younger children:* Children may hide behind a screen because they cannot keep from peeking.
• *For older children:* Use a variety of different objects or let the child make a sound. The other children try to guess what the sound is or locate the hidden object.

## HOW DID IT GO?
• Are the children's attention spans increasing?
• How did the children show creativity in making their own sounds?

## MATERIALS NEEDED

a small toy or ball

# Name Game

*Children will learn each other's names by playing a game.*

*Christian Values:* enhancing self-esteem; valuing each other
*Bible:* Psalm 100:3 (God made each of us special.)

## GETTING READY
• Provide a large area for children to stand in a circle

## HOW TO DO IT
• Talk to the children about how each feels more important and accepted when called by his or her name.
• Ask the children to stand in a circle with their hands behind them. Choose one or ask a volunteer to be "It."
• "It" walks outside the circle, puts the toy in the hands of a child, and says: "Hi, I'm José."
• The other child turns around and says: "Hi, I'm Kevin."
• They shake hands. Kevin, who has the toy now, becomes "It" and repeats the process.

## VARIATIONS
• *For younger children:* As you roll the ball to a child say: "This ball is for Kevin."
• Kevin rolls the ball back to the teacher, and the ball is rolled to another child.
• *For older children:* Play the ball game, but have the children call the name of a child and roll the ball to that person.

## HOW DID IT GO?
• Which of the children need more encouragement to participate?
• Children will need to play this game several times to remember all of the children's names.

# What Is the Number?

*Children will use their gift of mental abilities to learn their numbers.*

***Christian Values:*** enhancing self-esteem; developing God's gifts
***Bible:*** Genesis 1:27 (God created us with different gifts.)

## MATERIALS NEEDED

egg carton
button
marker

## GETTING READY
- Use the marker to write the numbers 1 to 12 in the bottom of the egg cups.
- Place the button in the egg carton.
- Close the lid.

## HOW TO DO IT
- Choose one child at a time to shake the egg carton.
- The child then opens the carton and identifies the number under the button.

## VARIATIONS
- Depending on the size of the group use several egg carton shakers.
- *For older children:* Have each child count a set of buttons to equal the number of the cup where the button landed.
- Label the egg cups with alphabet letters or colors for children to identify.

## HOW DID IT GO?
- Did you feel you adapted this math game to the level of your children?
- How could you make it more challenging the next time?

# What Is It?

**MATERIALS NEEDED**

a grocery bag or box
small familiar objects such
as buttons, crayons,
bottle caps, cotton balls

*Children will identify and name an object by feeling it.*

*Christian Values:* thanking God for our senses;
developing our sense of touch
*Bible:* Psalm 92:1 (Give thanks to God.)

## GETTING READY
• Choose a child to be "It."

## HOW TO DO IT
• Explain the rules of the game.
• Let "It" stand in front with his back to the group, his hands behind his back.
• Ask one child to get an object from the bag or box and place it in "It's" hands. If "It" can name the object by feeling it, have him choose the next "It."
• Thank God for the children's sense of touch and ways it helps people.

## VARIATIONS
• *For younger children:* Learn the meaning of "smooth" and "rough" by using feely cards. Choose a variety of smooth- and rough-textured objects to glue onto the feely cards.

## HOW DID IT GO?
• How did the children let you know how they felt about the game?
• If the children get restless from waiting, stop the game and promise the others they will get their turn another day.

# Find the Place

## MATERIALS NEEDED

three boxes, each large
enough for a child to sit
in
three balls of assorted
sizes

*Children will develop the ability to follow directions and identify locations.*

**Christian Values:** using God's gift of the mind; enhancing self-esteem
**Bible:** Ephesians 4:15 (We are to grow in every way.)

## GETTING READY
- Cut boxes so they are no more than 12 inches high.
- Place boxes where you have circle time.

## HOW TO DO IT
- Let children take turns following a single direction:
  "Tasha, sit in the *biggest* box."
  "Mike, stand *between* two boxes."
  "Lana, put the red ball in the *middle* box."

## VARIATIONS
- *For younger children:* Cut the boxes low enough for twos to climb into.
- Play the same game with a variety of objects: blocks of different colors, stuffed or plastic animals.
- *For older children:* Let a child give the directions and determine if the other child followed the instructions correctly.

## HOW DID IT GO?
- Which directions seemed familiar to the children? With which spatial terms do they need more practice?

## MATERIALS NEEDED

space for a large circle
picture cards of various
animals

# My Right Side Is Vacant

*Children will learn the concepts of left and right as they play a game from Brazil.*

*Christian Values:* valuing God's gift of learning; appreciating traditions of all people
*Bible:* Ephesians 4:15 (We are to grow up in every way.)

## GETTING READY
• Make up cards with pictures of various animals.

## HOW TO DO IT
• Have the children sit in a circle with one chair vacant.
• Show the picture cards and have the children name the animals. Give each player a card and help the child know the name of the animal.
• The person to the left of the empty chair says, "My right side is vacant. Come here, *Dog.*" The child who has a picture of a dog goes to sit in the empty chair, leaving his former chair empty. The child holds up the picture card to show that he or she is a *dog.*
• Continue the game with the child on the left of the newly vacated chair being "It."

## VARIATIONS
• Make several sets of cards to use when learning different concepts such as foods, colors, flowers, toys, and insects.
• Change the game by letting the empty seat be on the left side.
• *For older children:* Let the teacher name the "It." Then the child must call out either *left* or *right.* This game is more difficult.

## HOW DID IT GO?
• Are the children able to distinquish between left and right?
• Did the game help them understand that children around the world like to play games?

# Play "I Want a Friend"

*Children will promote friendship and a sense of community by playing a game.*

**Christian Values:** accepting and respecting others; showing love

**Bible:** Ephesians 4:25b, 32 (In the Christian community we belong to one another and show love to one another.)

---

**MATERIALS NEEDED**

song "I Want a Friend"

---

## GETTING READY
- Plan a space for a large circle.
- Sing the song several times.

## HOW TO DO IT
- Have the children join hands in a circle.
- Have one child skip, gallop, or walk around the inside of the circle while everyone sings the song.
- On the last phrase, the teacher names a person in the circle.
- The person in the center skips to the person named, shakes hands, and exchanges places.

## VARIATIONS
- *For younger children:* Let the child who is "It" name the "friend" instead of the teacher doing it.
- *For older children:* Let "It" choose a friend, and they skip as a pair.

## HOW DID IT GO?
- What evidence did you have that the children felt the warmth of Christian community?
- Which children were unable to participate in a game with rules?

### I Want a Friend

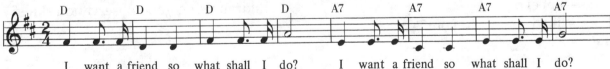

I want a friend so what shall I do? I want a friend so what shall I do?

I want a friend so what shall I do? I'll skip to my good friend *(name.)*

MUSIC: Traditional

**SOCIAL-EMOTIONAL RELATIONSHIPS • LARGE-MUSCLE SKILLS**

## MATERIALS NEEDED

# Sort the Children

*Children will sort and classify themselves by characteristics the leader names.*

**Christian Values:** enhancing self-esteem; affirming individual differences
**Bible:** Genesis 1:26 (Each person is created special.)

## GETTING READY
• Plan space for the children to sit and to stand in a circle.

## HOW TO DO IT
• Have children sit in a circle. Leader calls out characteristics and an action for those children to do:
  —All children wearing white shoes put your feet straight out in front of you.
• Suggested characteristics and actions to mix and match are
  colors of clothing—touch your nose
  eye color—stand up
  hair color—run in place
  ages—pat your back
  pets—kneel down
  foods liked—crawl to your seat

## VARIATIONS
• *For younger children:* Count and record the number of children in each classification.
• *For older children:* Make bar graphs of characteristics of children such as eye or hair colors.
• Use more difficult items to continue the game:
  freckles—jump three times
  types of clothing—touch your toes

## HOW DID IT GO?
• Did the children find it affirming to hear one of their characteristics called?
• In what ways did you observe the children using good observation skills?

# Who Has the Shoe?

*Children will play cooperatively in a game of hiding the shoe.*

**Christian Values:** relating to others; building trust; working cooperatively

**Bible:** Ephesians 4:25b (In the Christian community we belong to one another.)

## MATERIALS NEEDED

Shoes the children are wearing

## GETTING READY
• Prepare the sleeping space.

## HOW TO DO IT
• Children sit in a circle.
• One child is the sleeper and takes off one shoe. This child goes to a designated spot in the room and pretends to sleep with eyes closed.
• Another child is picked to hide the shoe by sitting on it. Everyone in the group must look as though they are hiding the shoe. No one is to tell.
• Wake the sleeper by calling: "——, ——, your shoe is gone. Oh where, oh where can it be?"
• The sleeper returns to the circle and tries to guess within three guesses who has the shoe.
• If the sleeper guesses correctly, the child hiding the shoe becomes the sleeper.

## VARIATIONS
• Place the shoe beside the sleeping space before the child goes to sleep. Pick another child to tiptoe to the shoe and return to the group to hide it.

## HOW DID IT GO?
• Were the children supportive of each other by not telling who had the shoe?
• Were the children able to wait patiently for a turn and to play cooperatively?

## MATERIALS NEEDED

blindfold

# Who Is Missing?

*Children will affirm everyone is important to the group by determining who is missing.*

*Christian Values:* understanding importance of each one in the community

*Bible:* Ephesians 4:25b (In the Christian community we belong to one another.)

## GETTING READY

- Plan space for the children to sit in a circle.
- Determine a good hiding place in the room.

## HOW TO DO IT

- Children sit in a circle.
- The child who is "It" is blindfolded and sits in the center of the circle.
- The leader asks a child to hide in a designated spot.
- "It" removes the blindfold and tries to guess who is missing.
- Depending on the age of the children, allow "It" to have one, two, or three guesses.
- When found, the missing child changes places with "It."

## VARIATIONS

- All children may change places after the child hides and before "It" begins guessing.
- (*A good variation for a visually handicapped child.*) "It" asks, "Who is missing?" and the missing child answers, "I am." "It" tries to guess from the voice who the child is.
- The Bible story "The Good Samaritan" would be good to use with this game.

## HOW DID IT GO?

- Did the children affirm each other and rejoice when the missing child was found?
- What evidence did you see that the children were involved in the game?

# Balance Beam

## MATERIALS NEEDED

balance beam
small objects such as bean
bags or flat rocks

*Children will learn to take turns and appreciate their developing large-muscle skills.*

*Christian Values:* enhancing self-esteem; valuing others
*Bible:* Psalm 100:3 (God made each one of us special.)

## GETTING READY
- Find the space to play.
- Collect the equipment.

## HOW TO DO IT
- When the children can walk the balance beam well, place two or three objects about 18 inches apart across the board.
- The children will step over the obstacles, trying not to lose their balance or have the foot touch the ground.
- Place two balance beams about 12 inches apart. Choose a pair of children to hold hands and walk the planks together. If one bobbles, they must both begin again. Encourage them to help each other.

## VARIATIONS
- *For younger children:* Twos will need you to hold their hands as they walk across the beam.

- *For older children:* Older children can use one of the objects to put on their heads and walk across the beam.
- Let children practice harder maneuvers by hopping across the beam, by walking sideways, or by placing the narrow side of the beam to walk on.

## HOW DID IT GO?
- What suggestions did the children make to have the game more challenging?
- How did you help the children feel special as they accomplished the skills at their own skill level?

**LARGE-MUSCLE SKILLS • SOCIAL-EMOTIONAL RELATIONSHIPS**

# Beanbag Toss

## MATERIALS NEEDED

a circle drawn on the
ground or a plastic pan
three beanbags per child

*Children will feel affirmed by participating in a
cooperative game.*

*Christian Values:* enhancing self-esteem;
respecting and accepting others
*Bible:* Psalm 25:4 (Teach me your ways, O God.)

## GETTING READY
- Choose a space to play.
- Make beanbags if necessary.
- Explain the game to the children.

## HOW TO DO IT
- Give each child three beanbags.
- Vary the throwing distance according to
  the age and skill of the children.
- Ask each child to try to toss each beanbag
  into the circle or plastic pan.
- Encourage all the children to applaud
  and affirm each toss.
- Let each child have a turn and then begin
  again.

## VARIATIONS
- *For younger children:* Children count as
  they toss the beanbags. They affirm
  themselves by clapping after each toss.
- *For older children:* Use this board for a
  thematic beanbag game such as a clown
  or a pumpkin toss: paint a picture on
  plywood or cardboard, leaving a hole to
  toss the beanbags through.

## HOW DID IT GO?
- How did the children show that they
  enjoyed the game?
- How was each child encouraged and
  supported in his or her efforts? How did
  the child respond?

# Walk the Plank

*Children will learn one way to care for their bodies by developing their large-muscle skills.*

*Christian Values:* strengthening our bodies; enhancing self-esteem
*Bible:* Luke 2:40 (Children grow today as Jesus grew.)

## MATERIALS NEEDED

one 8-foot long piece of 2 by 4 or 2 by 8 board, sanded smoothly

## GETTING READY
- Place a smoothly sanded walking board on the floor or on a level sidewalk.

## HOW TO DO IT
- Help children recall that God created our bodies. Discuss how to keep our bodies strong and healthy.
- Show the children how to walk on the balance beam. Demonstrate how to use your hands to keep your balance.
- Make a game by pretending that there is water on either side of the board. If a child falls off the board, pretend that he or she has wet feet.
- Encourage children to try different ways to step as they go across the board.

## VARIATIONS
- *For younger children:* Assist unsteady or younger children by holding their hand.
- Count each step aloud that is made on the board.
- *For older children:* Keep track of how many steps each child can make across the board without falling off or stepping on the floor. Avoid competition by applauding each child's efforts.
- Make the task more difficult by raising the board from the floor. Nail the board securely on a wooden block at each end.

## HOW DID IT GO?
- Was it hard for the younger children to balance? If so, place two boards side by side.
- Did the children trust that you would hold their hand if needed?

# Clothesline Game

## MATERIALS NEEDED

pinch-style clothespins
clothesline or heavy cord
doll clothes
paper
scissors
adhesive paper

*Children will make choices and complete a task by participating in a group activity.*

**Christian Values:** making choices; being responsible

**Bible:** 1 Corinthians 4:12a (We work with our hands.)

## GETTING READY

• Hang clothesline at the children's height. Be sure to fasten ends securely.
• Select doll clothes to use, or cut shapes out of paper: food, nature items, animal shapes. Select shapes that have either a matching shape or an associated shape (such as things you wear on your head).

## HOW TO DO IT

• At circle time have each child, in turn, find a pair of items to hang beside each other on the clothesline.
• Or let the teacher hang one item and have a child hang beside it a picture of something that is associated with that item, such as a hen and an egg.
• Let the child tell about his or her selection.

## VARIATIONS

• *For younger children:* Vary the game according to the experiences of the children. Young children will have more success at matching than at choosing go-together items.
• *For older children:* Let children cut their own shapes or clothes out of paper to hang.

## HOW DID IT GO?

• Did children have difficulty using clothespins? Do they need more hand-strengthening activities?

**THINKING SKILLS • SMALL-MUSCLE SKILLS**

# Do What I Do

## MATERIALS NEEDED

Use simple rhythm
instruments, if desired.

*Children will improve their listening skills by reproducing the leader's patterns of sound and action.*

**Christian Values:** enhancing self-esteem; sharing
with others
**Bible:** Psalm 100:1 (Make a joyful noise.)

## GETTING READY
- No preparation is needed, unless you use instruments.
- Use this game when you have times of transition or children need to wait in line.
- The younger the children, the simpler you make the patterns.

## HOW TO DO IT
- Clap a simple two-beat pattern.
- Children repeat the pattern.
- Vary the patterns with soft and loud claps or with rapid claps and long pauses.
- Increase to three- or four-clap patterns.
- Let children make a pattern for the class to follow.

## VARIATIONS
- *For younger children:* Add other motions: pat your head, slap your knee, stamp your feet, snap your fingers.
- *For older children:* Have the leader continue to add to the pattern until the group cannot duplicate it. Then start over.

## HOW DID IT GO?
- Were the children able to listen and follow the sequence?
- Note children who found this skill difficult. Plan for more follow-up later.

**THINKING SKILLS • SOCIAL-EMOTIONAL RELATIONSHIPS**

# Laundry Day

## MATERIALS NEEDED

a basket of assorted "laundry" for children— include several categories: pants, shirts, socks, towels, swimsuits laundry basket

*Children will learn comparison skills and classifying by sorting clothing.*

*Christian Values:* developing God's gift of mental abilities; learning to be helpful
*Bible:* Romans 12:4-7 (God has given us different gifts that can be used to help people.)

## GETTING READY

- Place the laundry basket on the floor and pile the clothing on the floor.

## HOW TO DO IT

- Tell children that today is "laundry day" and that they will be sorting the clothes for washing.
- Hold up one piece at a time and ask: "What is this? Where do we wear it?" Begin to put the clothes into piles according to what they are.
- After holding up several pieces, the children will begin to see similarities. On the second shirt, for example, ask: "Which pile does this go in?"
- Continue until all of the laundry is sorted by categories.

## VARIATIONS

- *For younger children:* Sort the laundry by color, by size, or by seasonal clothing.
- Make a small clothesline and leave some laundry in the housekeeping area for children to use in dramatic play.

## HOW DID IT GO?

- Did the children think of new and different ways to sort the laundry?
- What other things might the children sort?

# Letter Carrier

## MATERIALS NEEDED

used addressed envelopes
a mailbag
a letter carrier's hat

*Children will identify the letter carrier as a community worker who helps people.*

**Christian Values:** using God's gifts to help others; developing our talents
**Bible:** Genesis 1:27 (God created us with different gifts.)

## GETTING READY
- Make a mailbag from a heavy paper sack. Punch a hole on each side and tie a long heavy cord for a handle.
- Make a hat by stapling a narrow band to fit around a child's head. Glue or staple a bill on the front.
- Have children bring some old envelopes that have their address on it.

## HOW TO DO IT
- Discuss with the children how mail is delivered and how the letter carrier finds their home.
- Help children review their name and address.
- Choose one child to be the letter carrier who says: "I have some mail for ———" and reads the house numbers.
- The named child becomes the next letter carrier.

## VARIATIONS
- The letter carrier describes someone in the group. Other children try to guess from the description whom the mail is for.
- The letter carrier says who the child is. The child described gets to be the new letter carrier.

## HOW DID IT GO?
- Note how carefully the children could listen to, observe, and remember details about other children.

**LANGUAGE DEVELOPMENT • THINKING SKILLS**

# Pack-a-Toy

## MATERIALS NEEDED

boxes of various sizes
toys that fit in each of the
boxes

*Children will feel satisfaction by solving problems together.*

*Christian Values:* making choices; developing a sense of community

*Bible:* 1 Corinthians 3:9 (We are workers with God.)

## GETTING READY
- Carefully select toys and boxes in a variety of sizes and shapes.
- Put children into small groups.

## HOW TO DO IT
- The small group will work together to match toys with boxes that fit.
- Let children test their ideas by putting toys in the boxes. If a wrong choice is made, encourage child to try again.
- Children may have to remove all of the toys and start the process again until each box has a toy that fits.
- Game is completed when all toys have been placed in an appropriate box.

## VARIATIONS
- Play this game as you prepare to wrap gifts of toys or food for special mission projects.

## HOW DID IT GO?
- Did the boxes and toys selected challenge the children's thought, yet not frustrate them?

# Season Adventure

*Children will become aware of seasonal gifts that God provides.*

**Christian Values:** appreciating the wonder of God's creation; appreciating the orderliness of God's plan

**Bible:** Ecclesiastes 3:11 (God has made everything beautiful in its time.)

## MATERIALS NEEDED

masking tape
seasonal clothes
seasonal activity materials
seasonal foods
seasonal pictures

## GETTING READY

- Set up an obstacle course with opportunities to move over, under, through, between, and so on.
- Along the course place items that represent the season in your area (foods eaten, clothing worn, games played, nature changes).
- Display seasonal pictures at the eye level of the children.

## HOW TO DO IT

- Look at the pictures and discuss the season, what the people do, how nature looks, or the temperature.
- As children move through the course, let children ask questions about seasonal items: "What is this?" (soup); "What is the weather like when we like to eat hot soup?"; "What other foods can make us feel warm in the cold winter?"
- Thank God for the things we enjoy doing or eating during each season.

## VARIATIONS

- *For older children:* Use holiday traditions rather than seasonal objects.

## HOW DID IT GO?

- Could the children express praise to God for gifts of the season?

## MATERIALS NEEDED

cotton balls
small containers
liquids to smell such as
peppermint extract
perfume
orange juice
hot chocolate
strawberry flavor

# Smelling Game

*Children will sharpen their gift of smell by playing a game.*

*Christian Values:* enjoying the gift of smell; discovering God's world
*Bible:* Psalm 96:1 (Make a joyful noise to God.)

## GETTING READY

- Place a few drops of each fragrance on a different cotton ball. Place in small containers for children to hold and smell.
- Check for any children with allergies.

## HOW TO DO IT

- Pass around the different scented cotton balls for the children to identify.
- Give each child a cotton ball and let the child choose a fragrance to put on it.
- Each child tries to find someone who has the same scent he or she has.
- Remind the children that God has given each object a special smell that helps people identify objects or warns of danger, such as a fire.

## VARIATIONS

- Use only a small group of children to do this activity.
- Use other objects that children can hold and smell such as oranges, cinnamon sticks, or popcorn.

## HOW DID IT GO?

- How did the children respond as they searched for their scent?
- Which children had trouble in finding their scent? How will you help them?

# What Do You Hear?

*Children will use their senses as they identify sounds.*

**Christian Values:** appreciating God's gift of the senses; understanding God's world
**Bible:** Psalm 100 (Be thankful for God has made us.)

**MATERIALS NEEDED**

pictures of modern-day scenes involving children in various activities

## GETTING READY
• Find appropriate pictures for the game.
• Be ready to do an example with the children.

## HOW TO DO IT
• Gather the children around you so each one can see the pictures.
• Hold up a picture. Ask: "If you were looking out a window at this scene, what sounds would you hear?"
• You may name a sound first ("I think I would hear the birds singing.") Then encourage the children to give their answers.
• Change the picture after three or four children have responded. Repeat the process.

## VARIATIONS
• *For younger children:* Good books to read are *City Noisy Book* and *Country Noisy Book,* by Margaret W. Brown. Ask the children to repeat the sounds as you read the stories.
• *For older children:* Take a walk and let the children dictate a story, using sounds, that the teacher writes on newsprint.

## HOW DID IT GO?
• Were the children able to use their imagination? Could they recall sounds?
• Would you use this game again?

## MATERIALS NEEDED

any household materials
that make a noise—for
example:
  an egg beater
  scissors
  a bell
  Velcro on shoes

# What's That Sound?

*Children will enhance their listening and attention-span skills by playing a game of sounds.*

*Christian Values:* using God's gift of hearing; responding to nature
*Bible:* Acts 13:16 (People who love God learn to listen.)

## GETTING READY
- Hide materials so that the children cannot see them.
- Assemble children in a group on the floor or around the table.

## HOW TO DO IT
- Keep the objects hidden. Using one at a time, make a noise with each object. Ask if anyone knows what could make this sound.
- Accept all answers as a possibility, then reveal what the object is.
- There are no winners or losers; the game is played for fun.
- Help children identify sounds that are high or low, loud or soft, sweet or harsh.

## VARIATIONS
- On the next day for show and tell, encourage the children to bring an object from home. Let the child use it to make a noise while the others guess.

## HOW DID IT GO?
- Can the children really concentrate on one sound? Can they identify the object readily?
- Were they easily distracted by the quiet atmosphere?

# Indian Symbols

### MATERIALS NEEDED

2-inch wide strips of
  construction paper long
  enough to fit around
  child's head
crayons or markers
chart for display of
  symbols
stapler or tape
book of Indian symbols

*Children will become aware of one different culture in our country, and will grow in appreciation of the Native American culture.*

*Christian Values:* appreciating God's plan for people to be different; developing acceptance of all persons

*Bible:* Ephesians 2:19 (We are all members of the family of God.)

## GETTING READY
- Draw some Indian symbols on a large piece of paper.

## HOW TO DO IT
- Distribute strips of paper and crayons. Ask children to draw some symbols.
- Tell children that long ago Indian people used picture language to tell stories.
- Discuss each symbol and ask the children what they think it means. Tell the meaning of each symbol.
- Children may take turns "reading" their Indian symbols.
- Measure and staple, tape, or glue the strips to form headbands.

## VARIATIONS
- Create your own hand or body symbols to stand for words like water, trees, wind, run, and hop.
- *For older children:* These children might enjoy writing a story or letter using the symbols.

## HOW DID IT GO?
- Did the children learn about a different way to communicate?
- Did this activity help children to appreciate better the Native American culture?

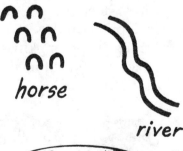
horse

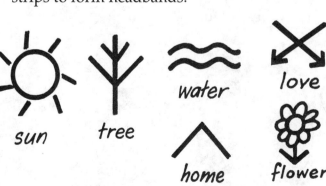
sun    tree    water    love    home    flower

man
or
friend

river

## MATERIALS NEEDED

various sizes of recycled
   paper bags
old newspapers
orange tempera paint
green tempera paint
string or green yarn
straw or hay (if available)

# The Pumpkin Patch

*Children will enjoy re-creating a pumpkin patch.*

*Christian Values:* appreciating God's creation;
   using God's gift of creativity
*Bible:* Psalm 9:1-2 (I will give thanks.)

## GETTING READY
- Show pictures of pumpkins or other crops growing on a vine.
- Bring a real pumpkin into the classroom.

## HOW TO DO IT
- Give children paper bags and allow them to stuff them with newspaper. Twist the top of the bag to make a stem and tie with green yarn.
- Allow children to paint the fat part of the pumpkin orange. Then paint the stem green. Let dry.
- Tie the pumpkins together, leaving about 1 to 1½ feet of string or yarn in between each pumpkin.
- Arrange the pumpkins in a corner or on a table covered with hay or straw.

## VARIATIONS
- Children may cut green leaves from construction paper and glue to the yarn stems to make a vine.
- Take the class on a field trip to see a farm in the fall or a pumpkin patch. Write a letter of thanks to the farmer.
- Thank God for the beauty of fall and for special foods that we have in the fall.
- Make a bulletin board using small pumpkins made from lunch bags.

## HOW DID IT GO?
- In what ways did children express appreciation for God's world in the fall? Can they identify a vine, a pumpkin, and other fall foods?

**CREATIVE ART • THINKING SKILLS**

# A Thanksgiving Litany

*Children will become aware of Thanksgiving Day and create a thank-you litany.*

**Christian Values:** expressing own feelings; praising God
**Bible:** Psalm 92:1 (Give thanks and sing praises to God.)

## MATERIALS NEEDED

large piece of newsprint
felt-tip marker
story about the biblical or modern Thanksgiving
construction paper, glue

## GETTING READY
- Choose a book or story about thanksgiving to read to the children.
- Gather supplies needed.

## HOW TO DO IT
- Read the book or story to the children.
- Talk with the group about what the word *thankful* means.
- In small groups, ask each child to tell one thing for which he or she is thankful. The teacher will write each idea on the paper.
- Write the response to each statement "We thank you, God." Use during your worship time.
- By the next class session, make a copy of the litany for each child to mount on construction paper and use at home on Thanksgiving Day.

## VARIATIONS
- *For younger children:* Ask each child what he or she is thankful for.
- *For older children:* If a helper is available, let each child create a litany.
- Have the children decorate covers for their litanies.
- Use the litany often as a prayer.

## HOW DID IT GO?
- Did you get some unusual responses for the litany?
- Were the children pleased that they could write a prayer?

For our food
We thank you, God.
For our families
We thank you, God.

# Christmas Star

## MATERIALS NEEDED

long bamboo skewers
glue
scissors
red or green yarn
construction paper
cardboard star patterns
glitter, bits of lace, tin foil
    to decorate stars

*Children will remember events in the Christmas story by making a star, an important symbol.*

*Christian Values:* remembering our Christian heritage; developing creativity
*Bible:* Matthew 2:1-10 (Wise men followed a star to find baby Jesus.)

## GETTING READY

- Cut bamboo skewers in thirds. Each child will need five sticks.
- Make cardboard star patterns.

## HOW TO DO IT

- Give every two or three children a cardboard star pattern.
- Have children lay their sticks on the star patterns. Glue the ends together to form the star frame. Remove the frame from the cardboard to dry.
- Let each child trace two patterns onto construction paper and cut them out. Encourage children to decorate their paper stars with sequins, glitter, lace, foil, and so on. When finished, glue the two paper stars onto the back and front of the frame.
- Punch a hole at one point, thread red or green yarn through it, and tie for hanging.
- Carry the star in your Christmas Eve parade (page 102).

## VARIATIONS

- *For younger children:* Children can decorate their stars with glue and glitter. Teachers will need to help them tape or tie the ends of the sticks together to form the star.

## HOW DID IT GO?

- This activity will be hard for young children. How did the children respond to the frustration of doing a hard task?
- Did you sense appreciation for the fact that many cultures have similar Christmas celebrations and symbols?

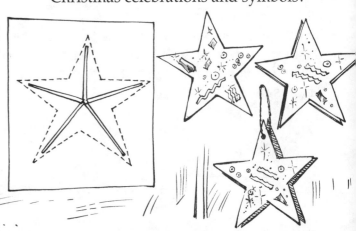

# Mexican Ornament

*Children will celebrate Christmas by making a Mexican-style metal ornament.*

*Christian Values:* celebrating our heritage; understanding Christians around the world
*Bible:* Luke 2:10-11 (I bring good news of great joy for all the people: to you is born this day a Savior.)

## MATERIALS NEEDED

aluminum foil
art tissue paper
white glue
small brushes
yarn

## GETTING READY
- Cut foil into circles, squares, triangles, and rectangles about 4 inches in size.
- Tear tissue paper into ½- to 1-inch pieces

## HOW TO DO IT
- Brush foil pieces with glue.
- Arrange tissue-paper pieces on the foil shapes.
- Encourage children to leave some foil on the edges to fold over the tissue.
- Let dry. Punch a hole in top and tie yarn to make a hanger.

## VARIATIONS
- Use foil cupcake wrappers. Children smooth them out flat.
- Help the children relate this art activity to the celebration of Christmas in Mexico.

## HOW DID IT GO?
- Did the children show pride in making the ornaments?
- In what ways did the children show that they understand what Christmas is?

# Mitten Christmas Tree

## MATERIALS NEEDED

green and brown
  construction paper
mittens children bring
tape
pushpins

*Children will celebrate Christmas by sharing mittens with persons in need.*

*Christian Values:* loving and sharing with one another; remembering our Christian heritage
*Bible:* Acts 2:46 (Members of the Christian family share with one another.)

## GETTING READY

- On a bulletin board make a large Christmas tree from green construction paper.
- Find out where you can send mittens for needy children.
- In a letter to parents explain the mitten project. Give a date when you want children to bring them.

## HOW TO DO IT

- Tell children that one good way of celebrating Christmas is by giving gifts.
- Tell them about children who need mittens. Say: "Let's make a happy Christmas for them. We can decorate this Christmas tree with new mittens that each of you bring. We will pack these and send them to needy children."
- Send the letters home.
- Let each child hang his or her mittens on the tree.

## VARIATIONS

- Cut out pictures from old greeting cards and decorate the box to put the mittens in.
- Older children may help deliver the gifts.

## HOW DID IT GO?

- Did everyone bring mittens?
- How did the older children feel about the children they visited?

# Reindeer Sandwiches

*Children will celebrate the Christmas season by making a reindeer sandwich.*

*Christian Values:* enhancing self-esteem; using
   creative abilities
*Bible:* Matthew 14:16 (Jesus recognized the need
   for persons to share food.)

## MATERIALS NEEDED

whole-wheat bread
peanut butter
raisins
cherries
pretzel sticks
plastic knives for children
toaster
small paper plates
wet paper towels

## GETTING READY
- Assemble ingredients.
- Toast bread, remove crust, and cut into
   four triangles. Save crust for birds.
- Cut cherries in halves.

## HOW TO DO IT
- Give each child a small paper plate with
   two triangles of toast.
- Spread peanut butter on each triangle.
- Decorate with raisins for eyes, a half
   cherry for a nose, and pretzel sticks for
   antlers.

## VARIATIONS
- *For older children:* Children may cut their
   own triangles of bread.
- Use homemade peanut butter, if made
   earlier. See page 58.
- Use the reindeer sandwich to introduce
   the letter *R*.

## HOW DID IT GO?
- Did the children enjoy the creativity of
   their snack?
- Which children were not able to follow
   directions?
- Did all children work well together as a
   group, learning to share and take turns?

## MATERIALS NEEDED

Christmas stars (see page 98)
newsprint
felt-tip marker
Christmas music

# Star Parade

*Children will participate in a custom from the Philippines.*

*Christian Values:* respecting and appreciating Christmas traditions from other cultures

*Bible:* Matthew 2:2 (We have seen his star and have come to worship him.)

## GETTING READY

- Print the words "Maligayang Pasko" on newsprint.
- Make space to have a parade.

## HOW TO DO IT

- Tell the children about this Filipino custom. Say: "In many towns in the Philippines, people make elaborate lanterns shaped like stars. On Christmas Eve these are lighted and carried in a parade through the town to recall the story of the wise men who came to see Jesus."
- Practice saying "Merry Christmas" in Pilipino (mah-lee-guy-ung pahs-koh).
- Have children hold up the stars they made as they parade around the room.

## VARIATIONS

- *For older children:* Let them tie their stars to dowels to carry in the parade.
- Sing "Maligayang Pasko" to the tune of "Happy Birthday to You."

## HOW DID IT GO?

- Did the children enjoy participating in a custom from another culture?
- Did the older children enjoy singing in another language to help them be aware that people in other countries also celebrate Christmas?

# Straw Ornaments

*Children will celebrate Christmas by making ornaments to use at home or to share with others.*

**Christian Values:** remembering our Christian heritage; sharing with others
**Bible:** Hebrews 13:16 (Do not forget to share.)

## MATERIALS NEEDED

three different-colored drinking straws for each child
scissors
yarn
glue

## GETTING READY
- Make a sample to show the class.

## HOW TO DO IT
- Demonstrate how to make the straw ornament.
- Let the children choose what color straws and yarn they want to use.
- Ask the children to cut each straw in half.
- Teachers or another child may help them tie all the straws together in the middle, very tightly, with yarn. The straws can be spread out like a circle.
- Hang the ornaments by tying a piece of yarn in the middle to make a hanger loop.

## VARIATIONS
- To make a Christmas tree chain, children can alternately string a piece of drinking straw, a star or flower cut from construction paper, a drinking straw, and so on.
- Purchase craft straws at a hobby shop and let the children make Mexican star ornaments using the same steps as above.

## HOW DID IT GO?
- Did you provide enough colors for the children to make choices?

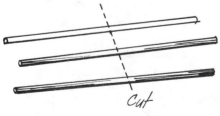

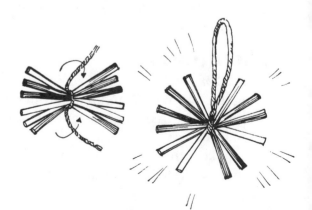

## MATERIALS NEEDED

green construction paper
masking tape
yellow star
brown base for tree
scissors

# Wall Christmas Tree

*Children will help celebrate Christmas by decorating their classroom.*

*Christian Values:* celebrating the birth of Jesus; valuing our Christmas tradition
*Bible:* Psalm 100:1 (Make a joyful noise.)

## GETTING READY
• Assemble your materials.
• Cut paper into 1- by 9-inch strips.

## HOW TO DO IT
• Show the young children how to snip (or fringe) one side of the green strips.
• Distribute one or two strips for each child to do.
• Outline a triangle on a bulletin board or large sheet of paper on the wall. Children will glue their finished strips within the tree outline.
• Cut a base for the tree out of brown construction paper. Glue the star on top.

## VARIATIONS
• Make paper chains. Tie six or eight chains together at the top and hang from the point of the tree. Glue or tape the star at the top. Separate the chains at the bottom to make a tree shape and tape each end in place. Make a brown tub for the base.

## HOW DID IT GO?
• Were the children proud of the tree they made?
• What evidences of cooperation did the children show?

**SMALL-MUSCLE SKILLS • MATH READINESS**

# New Year's Balloon Collage

*Children will express their thanks to God for the beginning of a new year.*

*Christian Values:* praising God; expressing creativity

*Bible:* Galatians 4:10 (We observe days, months, seasons, and years.)

## MATERIALS NEEDED

assorted colors of
   construction paper
school glue
scissors
small brushes
confetti or a paper punch
thin string streamers
yarn
glitter

## GETTING READY
- Cut construction paper into a balloon shape for each child.
- Use water to thin the glue.
- Use a paper punch to make confetti (or let children do it).

## HOW TO DO IT
- Brush a thin coat of glue over the balloon shape.
- Sprinkle the confetti and glitter on the balloons.
- Glue the streamers over the confetti to make a design.
- Dry flat.
- Tie a yarn string to the balloon.

## VARIATIONS
- Group balloons together on a bulletin board and tie with a big bow.
- *For older children:* Talk about resolutions. Have children make a statement of some way they want to show love this year. Write the resolution on a small piece of paper and tie it to the balloon.
- Use the same technique to make a firework's collage for the Fourth of July.

## HOW DID IT GO?
- Did the children enjoy using their creativity in making the collage?
- Could older children make resolutions of ways to show love that were achievable at their age level?

**CREATIVE ART • LANGUAGE DEVELOPMENT**

## MATERIALS NEEDED

roll of white butcher paper
tempera paints: brown,
   yellow, pink, tan (white
   and brown)
pie pans
scissors
green marker
picture or book about King

# Friendship Mural

*Children will celebrate Martin Luther King's birthday by learning that we all belong to God's family.*

*Christian Values:* accepting all people; relating to others
*Bible:* John 15:17 (Love one another.)

## GETTING READY
• Cut white paper into large globe.
• Sketch land forms on globe with green marker.
• Prepare four colors of paint in pie pans for handprints.

## HOW TO DO IT
• Discuss how children are different: size, color of eyes, families, interests.
• Discuss how children are alike: they love, share, express kindness, wish, dream.
• Show King's picture and tell about his dream that all people could live together in peace and love.
• Make a Friendship Mural by having children dip hands in paint and making a print on the globe. Touch fingers for friendship.

## VARIATIONS
• Make Friendship Mural place mats.
• Children identify ways they can show love with their hands. Record list.
• Show pictures of different ways children can express love.

## HOW DID IT GO?
• Do you feel that the discussion affirmed each child's uniqueness?
• What evidence did you observe that the children understood ways to express love with their hands?

**SOCIAL-EMOTIONAL RELATIONSHIPS**

# Hello, Mr. Groundhog!

*Children will learn about one of God's animals and hear about Groundhog Day.*

*Christian Values:* appreciating God's animal world and God's plan for weather and seasons
*Bible:* Genesis 1:31 (God saw everything that he had made, and indeed, it was very good.)

## MATERIALS NEEDED

4- or 6-ounce paper cups
craft sticks
pattern of a groundhog

## GETTING READY
- Prepare to tell the legend about Groundhog Day.
- Make a groundhog face for each child.
- Make a slit in the bottom of each cup.

## HOW TO DO IT
- Tell the legend of the groundhog.
- Distribute a pattern of a groundhog to each child. Let children color it.
- Let children glue the pattern to the top of a craft stick.
- Insert the stick into a small slit in the bottom of a paper cup. Pull the stick down so that the groundhog's head is hidden.
- Push the stick up to make the groundhog "pop up" out of his hole.

## VARIATIONS
- Add grass around the rim of the cup by fringing light brown construction paper and gluing it in place.
- Use the puppet cup for children to retell the legend of the groundhog.
- Play a game for Groundhog Day. Describe the weather each time and let the children be the groundhog and respond appropriately.

## HOW DID IT GO?
- Did the children show an interest in learning more about the groundhog?
- Could children tell the meaning of being able to see the groundhog on February 2?

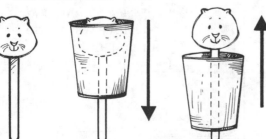

**SCIENCE DEVELOPMENT • LANGUAGE DEVELOPMENT**

**107**

## MATERIALS NEEDED

three red hearts
scissors
felt-tip pens
crayons

# Three Little Valentines

*Children will learn about loving others by saying a fingerplay.*

*Christian Values:* loving others; enhancing self-esteem

*Bible:* 1 John 4:19 (We love because God first loved us.)

## GETTING READY
- Cut three hearts out of construction paper or paint three hearts on large paper.

## HOW TO DO IT
- Have the children gather together in the circle time area.
- Show the three valentines to the children and then teach the fingerplay with motions.
- Let older children draw faces on the valentines.

## VARIATIONS
- *For younger children:* Teachers may draw the faces on the valentines for the children.
- Change the names in the fingerplay to names of children in the class.
- Choose three children to walk hand in hand while the class says the fingerplay.

## HOW DID IT GO?
- Did you and the children feel God's love as you said the fingerplay?

**Three Little Valentines**

Three little valentines
 walking hand in hand
(*use fingers to "walk" on hand*)
Spreading God's love
 all over our land
(*spread arms wide*)
A hug for Billy
 and a kiss for Lei
(*hug self and throw a kiss*)
God's love was made
 for you and me!
(*point to someone, then to self*)

# Valentine Sandwiches

*Children will celebrate Valentine's Day as a day of love by making valentine sandwiches to share.*

*Christian Values:* sharing with others; using the gift of creativity
*Bible:* 1 John 4:7 (Love one another.)

## MATERIALS NEEDED

slices of white bread
heart-shaped cookie
  cutters
cream cheese
red fruit jelly
paper towels
plastic knives and
  teaspoons

## GETTING READY
- Ask another adult to assist.

## HOW TO DO IT
- Talk about sharing as one way to show others God's love. Encourage children to talk about special people in their lives whom they love and want to share love with (a parent, neighbor, relative).
- Let two children give each person a paper towel and a slice of white bread.
- Show children how to use the cookie cutter. Let them take turns cutting out their heart-shaped bread. Spread cream cheese on top. Add a dab of red fruit jelly.

## VARIATIONS
- *For older children:* Use soft tacos instead of bread. Sprinkle grated cheese on top. Heat in the oven until cheese melts.
- Make enough sandwiches to invite another class to join in your valentine celebration.

## HOW DID IT GO?
- How did the activity promote friendship and sharing between the classes?
- What evidence of cooperation was there in preparing the food?

## MATERIALS NEEDED

empty paper-towel rolls or
  bathroom-tissue rolls
brown tempera paint
brown paper
glue or staples
paintbrushes
painting aprons

# Abe Lincoln's Cabin

*Children will celebrate President's Day, create a log cabin, and hear stories about Abraham Lincoln.*

*Christian Values:* using our gift of creativity; valuing others
*Bible:* Hebrews 13:16 (Do good and help one another.)

## GETTING READY
• Prepare to tell a story about Abraham Lincoln and what life was like when he lived.
• Collect pictures of log cabins.

## HOW TO DO IT
• Tell a story about the life of Abraham Lincoln.
• Show children how to paint the empty towel rolls. Allow them to dry. Staple them on a bulletin board or on stiff posterboard to make a log cabin.
• Cut brown paper into squares to make shingles for the roof. Glue in place overlapping each one. The size will depend on the size of the cabin.

## VARIATIONS
• *For younger children:* Use commercial toy logs for building a cabin.
• *For older children:* Use the logs to cover a cardboard box to make a dramatic-play cabin. Pretend to sleep on the floor, read books, or cook outside.

## HOW DID IT GO?
• Were the children able to work together cooperatively and to share?
• How did the children resolve problems?

# Easy Cherry Crisp

*Children will enjoy working together to make a special snack treat.*

**Christian Values:** sharing and taking turns; working together
**Bible:** Matthew 14:16 (Jesus recognized the need for persons to share food.)

## MATERIALS NEEDED

recipe ingredients
oven
9-by-13 baking pan
small mixing bowl
fork, teaspoon
measuring cup
mixing spoon
small cups and spoons

## GETTING READY

- Assemble ingredients on a low table where the children can work.
- Preheat oven to 350 degrees.
- Open cans of cherry filling.
- Lightly grease the baking pan.

## HOW TO DO IT

- Let two children pour the cans of pie filling into the baking pan.
- Take turns blending the flour and butter in the bowl with a fork.
- Let other children measure and add sugar, brown sugar, and cinnamon.
- Children mix well. Sprinkle mixture over the cherries.
- Bake for 30 minutes.

## VARIATIONS

- Plan to use this food to celebrate George Washington's birthday.
- Use other fruits such as apples, peaches, or blueberries.

## HOW DID IT GO?

- Did all the children feel they participated in the preparation?
- Could the children patiently take turns?
- Did you see evidence of good self-esteem for having made something themselves?

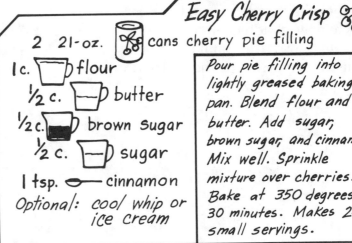

Easy Cherry Crisp

2 21-oz. cans cherry pie filling
1 c. flour
½ c. butter
½ c. brown sugar
½ c. sugar
1 tsp. cinnamon
Optional: cool whip or ice cream

Pour pie filling into lightly greased baking pan. Blend flour and butter. Add sugar, brown sugar, and cinnamon. Mix well. Sprinkle mixture over cherries. Bake at 350 degrees for 30 minutes. Makes 24 small servings.

## MATERIALS NEEDED

palm fronds
construction paper
scissors
items for making musical
  instruments such as:
    oatmeal boxes
    aluminum pie pans
    tape, pebbles
    dowels
    bells, elastic

# Palm Sunday Parade

*Children will celebrate the events of Palm Sunday by acting them out.*

*Christian Values:* remembering Jesus and Palm Sunday; celebrating our faith
*Bible:* Mark 11:1-10 (Jesus entered Jerusalem.)

## GETTING READY

- Gather or make palm fronds.
- Practice telling the Palm Sunday story.
- Plan where you will have the parade.
- Decide whether to sing or just say "Hosanna!" during the parade.

## HOW TO DO IT

- Help children make drums, shakers or tambourines, sticks, and bells.
- Talk about the word *hosanna* as an expression of praise.
- Give some children instruments and the other children palm fronds.
- While the children parade, encourage them to wave the palm leaves, play instruments, sing or shout "Hosanna!"

## VARIATIONS

- *For younger children:* Use a stick horse to let children take turns riding the donkey.
- *For older children:* Have them make palm fronds from green construction paper. Roll the paper to within 3 inches of the end. Insert a second sheet and roll it within 3 inches of the end. Insert a third sheet, and roll all the way. Tape the roll at one end and make several cuts lengthwise in the roll. Pull paper gently from the center outward. Crimp the bottom to make a handle.

## HOW DID IT GO?

- What evidence did you see that the children know the Palm Sunday story?

**MUSIC • LARGE-MUSCLE SKILLS**

# Easter Bunny Card

*Children will learn about and celebrate Easter in both Christian and secular ways by making an Easter bunny card.*

*Christian Values:* enhancing self-esteem; being creative; remembering our Christian heritage
*Bible:* Acts 3:15 (God raised Jesus from the dead.)

## MATERIALS NEEDED

light cardboard
paper fasteners
crayons or markers
scissors
paper punch

## GETTING READY
- Draw the patterns for two egg shapes per child on light cardboard.
- Draw a line lengthwise down the middle of one egg.

## HOW TO DO IT
- Give each child two cardboard egg patterns. Help the children cut out the eggs and cut one apart on the line. The cut pieces become the ears.
- Have the children decorate both sides of the ears.
- The second egg becomes the face of the rabbit. Color eyes, nose, mouth, and whiskers.
- Write each child's message on the back of the face.
- Hold the ears at the top of the message side. Punch a hole and let the children attach the ears with a paper fastener.
- When the ears are separated, the Easter message will be revealed.

## VARIATIONS
- *For younger children:* Teachers may cut out the patterns for very young children and draw the features on the face, which the children can color.
- *For older children:* Let children draw and cut their own egg shapes. Most can decorate them and write their own message.
- Older children can make the cards in different sizes and then arrange them according to size.

## HOW DID IT GO?
- How much creativity did the children show in decorating?

**SMALL-MUSCLE SKILLS • CREATIVE ART**

# Bunny Salad

## MATERIALS NEEDED

for each child:
- 1 pear half
- 2 raisins
- 1 red gumdrop
- 2 slices of banana
- 1 teaspoon of cottage cheese
- 1 lettuce leaf

toothpicks, small paper plates, napkins, plastic forks

*Children will enjoy creating a delicious snack from foods God created.*

**Christian Values:** developing creativity; enjoying God's world

**Bible:** Genesis 1:11-12 (God made the plants and trees.)

## GETTING READY
- Assemble ingredients and supplies.
- Make a model bunny to show.
- Wash vegetables. Pull lettuce leaves apart.

## HOW TO DO IT
- Show ingredients to the children. Discuss where each ingredient comes from. (Pears from trees, bananas from trees, lettuce from a plant.)
- Have children make their own bunny.
  a. Give each child a paper plate.
  b. Put a lettuce leaf on the plate.
  c. Lay the pear, rounded side up, on the leaf.
  d. Put the gumdrop at the tip of the small end of the pear for the nose.
  e. Place raisins for the eyes.
  f. Cut the banana in half; then cut it lengthwise to form two ears.
  g. Use a dab of cottage cheese for the tail.

## VARIATIONS
- *For younger children:* Adults will need to help in assembling the bunny.

## HOW DID IT GO?
- Did the children know where each food came from?
- Were the children willing to taste any new foods?

**THINKING SKILLS • SOCIAL-EMOTIONAL RELATIONSHIPS**

# Make an Easter Egg

*Children will celebrate Easter and express their creativity by making a water color egg.*

*Christian Values:* expressing God's gift of creativity; celebrating Easter
*Bible:* Ecclesiastes 3:11 (God has made everything beautiful.)

## MATERIALS NEEDED

water color paints
brushes
small cups of water
white typing paper
assorted spring colors of
  construction paper
glue
newspaper

## GETTING READY
- Cover work space with newspaper.
- Cut a large oval egg shape out of construction paper for each child.
- Gather needed supplies.

## HOW TO DO IT
- Talk with the children about the meaning of new life in the springtime when Easter comes.
- Take a walk and enjoy the beauty and colors of the outdoors in the spring.
- Children will freely paint the whole sheet of white paper with water colors.
- Avoid using black or brown. Observe the blending of the other spring colors.
- When the paint is dry, glue the egg shape mat over the painted paper.

## VARIATIONS
- *For younger children:* Use a half sheet of paper. Use markers for coloring.

## HOW DID IT GO?
- Did you see evidence of delight when the children viewed their creations?

**CREATIVE ART • SMALL-MUSCLE SKILLS**

# Maypole Dance

## MATERIALS NEEDED

1-inch by 3-foot dowel
fabric strips, ribbon, or
   streamer paper
long tack
record or tape player

*Children will participate in a group celebration experience.*

**Christian Values:** cooperating with others; expressing joy
**Bible:** Psalm 150:3-6 (Praise God with instruments and dance.)

## GETTING READY

- Cut ribbon, paper, or 1-inch wide fabric strips into 12-foot streamers. Make one for each two children.
- Securely tack the center of all strips to the end of the dowel.

## HOW TO DO IT

- Have a teacher stand in the middle of the circle of children to hold the dowel as children go around the circle. The teacher will need to turn slowly as the children go around.
- Call out movements for the children to make as they walk to the music going around the circle and holding the ribbon: reach high, bend low, flap arms.

## VARIATIONS

- Let those children not participating in the dance sit in chairs around the circle and sing favorite songs or clap to music played for the dance.
- Change groups often so all have a turn to do both types of activities.

## HOW DID IT GO?

- Were the children able to cooperate and look out for each other when moving in close circle?

# Arbor Day Fun

Children will celebrate Arbor Day by exploring God's gift of trees.

**Christian Values:** caring for God's creation; understanding the orderliness of God's plan
**Bible:** Psalm 75:1 (We give thanks to you, O God.)

## MATERIALS NEEDED

large sheet of mural paper
assorted small paper and
  wood items, pictures of
  foods from trees
glue
shovel
tree to plant

## GETTING READY
- Cut mural paper into large tree shape.
- Obtain permission and purchase the tree to plant.
- Display objects from trees.

## HOW TO DO IT
- Talk about the meaning of Arbor Day. Recall some of the traditions observed, especially ones in your community.
- Look through the collection of items from trees: paper, food, and wood items you have collected.
- Discuss the many ways trees help us (shade, food, beauty, windbreak, wood, fun, fresh air, homes for animals).
- Plant a small tree (or plant) at school and let the children be responsible for its care.

## VARIATIONS
- Sort the items before gluing. Lay the mural tree on the floor or long table and have the children glue the items on it. Let the mural dry thoroughly before you hang it.
- Go outdoors and examine some trees with magnifying glasses.

## HOW DID IT GO?
- What awareness of the values of trees did the children show?
- Did children grasp the idea of a need to save and care for trees?

## MATERIALS NEEDED

nature items
pictures of endangered
  species of animals
small table and cover
Bible
cardboard tubes
people figures from
  packets
cellophane tape
glue

# Ecology Worship Center

*Children will participate in prayer and praise as they think about special needs.*

**Christian Values:** caring for God's creation; living as God's people
**Bible:** 1 Corinthians 3:9 (We are workers with God.)

## GETTING READY
• Make figures by cutting pictures of animals from a magazine. Glue to a 2-inch cardboard tube to stand.
• Arrange your worship center.

## HOW TO DO IT
• Talk about God's gift of animals and our care of them.
• Talk about today's loss of forests and jungles for animals to live in safely and to have a good food and water supply.
• Have children place figures on the worship table. Compose a group prayer for people to care for God's world and the animals.

## VARIATIONS
• Place family figures on the worship center. Be sure to have a variety of adults and children representing different races. Encourage children to tell about their family members and how they care for them. Say sentence prayers or sing a prayer song thanking God for those persons.

## HOW DID IT GO?
• Were the children familiar with all of the animals on the altar?
• Could they identify persons in their lives and ways they care for them?

# Fancy Soaps

### MATERIALS NEEDED

Ivory Snow
water
food coloring
mixing bowl
large spoon
wax paper
plastic zipper bags
ribbon
newspapers

*Children will make a gift for Mom or Dad.*

*Christian Values:* expressing love and
   appreciation; using God's gifts for others
*Bible:* Ephesians 6:1-2 (Children should obey
   and honor their mothers and fathers.)

## GETTING READY
• Gather materials

## HOW TO DO IT
• Tint water with desired color.
• Stir ½ cup of tinted water to about two
  cups of Ivory Snow.
• On wax paper mold mixture into balls or
  other shapes.
• Let dry several days.
• Wrap the soaps in tissue paper and place
  in zipper bags.

## VARIATIONS
• Make soaps into small balls and package
  in a baby-food jar. Tie a ribbon around
  the jar top.

## HOW DID IT GO?
• Were the children looking forward to
  giving their gifts to their moms or
  dads?
• Were children creative in choosing their
  shapes and designs to use?

<table>
<tr><td>

**MATERIALS NEEDED**

  instant vanilla pudding
    mix and milk
  rotary egg beater
  fresh fruit (blueberries and
    strawberries)
  4- or 6-ounce clear plastic
    cups
  posterboard, markers
  paper towels, sponges
  tablespoons
  plastic knives

</td><td>

# Fourth of July Parfaits

*Children will become aware of traditional symbols as they celebrate special holidays.*

*Christian Values:* enjoying freedom; affirming
  uniqueness and value of each person
*Bible:* Psalm 75:1 (We give thanks to you, O
  God.)

</td></tr>
</table>

## GETTING READY

- Make a recipe chart using a pudding box and fruit pictures on posterboard.

## HOW TO DO IT

- Help children read the recipe and follow the directions to make pudding.
- Have children wash the fresh fruit and cut the strawberries.
- In a clear glass, place a layer of pudding, a layer of strawberries, another layer of pudding, and then some blueberries to make a festive red, white, and blue dessert.
- As children eat, talk about the meanings of the Fourth of July celebration and how people celebrate in different ways.
- Offer a prayer of thanksgiving to God for our nation and for our freedom to go to church.

## VARIATIONS

- If fresh fruit is not available, use canned pie filling (blueberry and cherry). Use can labels to make the recipe chart.
- Select other colors and fruit combinations for other holidays.

## HOW DID IT GO?

- Were children familiar with any other red, white, and blue American symbols?

Fourth of July Parfait
PREPARATION
Make the [pudding box]. Follow directions on box.
Wash [strawberries] and [blueberries].
Cut [strawberries].
MAKE DESSERT
In [cup] put a layer of [pudding].
Add a layer of [strawberries].
Add more [pudding].
Add [blueberries].

# Bird Naps

*Children will learn about some of God's creatures and the care they need.*

***Christian Values:*** respecting creation; understanding our responsibility
***Bible:*** Genesis 2:19 (God created all kinds of birds.)

## MATERIALS NEEDED

boxes large enough for three children to sit in
old blankets, sheets, and towels
nesting materials such as string, straw, towels, blankets, cotton
shovel and pan

## GETTING READY
- Line boxes with nesting materials.
- Invite extra adults to help today.
- Contact a parent to bring a pet bird.
- Locate record and record player.

## HOW TO DO IT
- Talk about some ways parent birds care for their baby birds.
- Encourage roleplay. Build a nest, teach birds how to fly, get food for them, keep them warm, let them nap.
- If you have the Age 2 Summer record, play "Baby Birds" and act out the motions.
- Say a thank-you prayer for God's wonderful creation and for all the things birds can do.

## VARIATIONS
- *For younger children:* Invite a family to bring a pet bird in a cage. (Check allergies.)
- *For older children:* Cut large holes in each side of a large box to make a cage. String yarn from top to bottom to make bars. Use a bench for a perch.
- Choose one child to be a bird. Have other children sing sounds to the bird and have the bird echo their sounds.

## HOW DID IT GO?
- Could the children follow instructions to do the motions of the song?
- Did you see the children caring for the bird in positive ways?

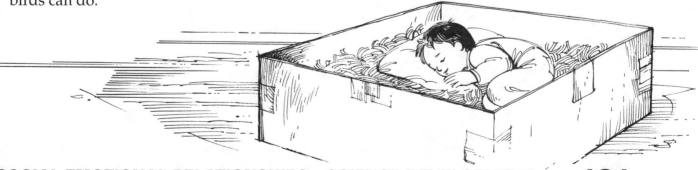

**SOCIAL-EMOTIONAL RELATIONSHIPS • SCIENCE DEVELOPMENT**

121

# Baby Birds

## MATERIALS NEEDED

song "Baby Birds"
record player
space for the children to
pretend to be birds

*Children will become sensitive to God's creatures by pretending to be birds.*

***Christian Values:*** understanding and caring for God's creation
***Bible:*** Matthew 6:26 (Jesus said to look at the birds.)

## GETTING READY
• Be able to sing the song.

## HOW TO DO IT
• Introduce the song: listen once and then sing it with the children.
• Ask one child to pretend to be the mother bird. Show how to keep her babies warm. Show the remaining children how to pretend they are baby birds.
• Play the song to help the children know when to be sleeping, to fly away, and to return. Act it out with the music.

## VARIATIONS
• Use the autoharp or piano instead of the record player.
• *For older children:* Let children create their own movements.

## HOW DID IT GO?
• Did the children understand how mother birds care for their babies?
• Which children seemed most comfortable with movement activities?
• How can you help children who seemed to be uncomfortable?

### Baby Birds

1. Ba - by birds a - sleep in a nest, Moth - er will keep you warm.
2. Ba - by birds, get out of the nest, It's time to fly a - round.
3. Ba - by birds, come back to your nest, Moth - er is wait - ing here;

Heads tucked un - der feath - er - y wings, Moth - er will keep you from harm.
Fly up high with feath - er - y wings, Now come back down to the ground.
Here they come on feath - er - y wings, Back to their moth - er so dear.

WORDS: Bette Atherton (stanza 1); Chloe Clark (stanzas 2 and 3) • MUSIC: Bette Atherton
Words (stanza 1) and music © 1964 by Graded Press; words (stanzas 2 and 3) © 1969 by Graded Press

# Caring for Pets

## MATERIALS NEEDED

stuffed dog, cat, and bird
dog or cat dish
birdcage
empty cans or boxes of
   dog, cat, and bird food
collar and leash for stuffed
   dog
toys for pets

*Children will roleplay caring for pets.*

*Christian Values:* learning to appreciate and care
   for God's creatures
*Bible:* Genesis 1:26b (People are to care for the
   animals God created.)

## GETTING READY
- Gather the pet props needed.
- Place them in the family living center.

## HOW TO DO IT
- Talk with the children about how they
   care for their pets.
- Show the props and demonstrate how
   you might use them.
- Let children pretend to feed the pet, give
   it a drink, brush its hair, take it for a
   walk, or play with it.
- Encourage children to tell each other
   about any pets they have and how they
   care for them.

## VARIATIONS
- Set up a pretend animal clinic.
- Plan for real pets to visit the classroom.
   Check with parents for any fears or
   allergies children may have. Check for
   any safety precautions you need to know
   about the pet.
- Use this activity with a unit on pets.

## HOW DID IT GO?
- Did the children show loving care for
   their pretend pets?
- Did they incorporate their pet play with
   their family-life play?

**SOCIAL-EMOTIONAL RELATIONSHIPS • SCIENCE DEVELOPMENT**

## MATERIALS NEEDED

a chair for each child
headphones
pretend instrument panel
pretend airline tickets
seat assignment cards
dress-up clothes for pilots
small suitcases or satchels

# Fly Away

*Children will discover and thank God for flying as one way to travel.*

*Christian Values:* appreciating God's gift of flight; enjoying God's world
*Bible:* Psalm 75:1 (We give thanks to you, O God.)

## GETTING READY
• Set up the chairs in rows to resemble seating on an airline. Number the seats.
• Set up a chair for the pilot and copilot.
• Make airline tickets and boarding passes.
• Draw dials and knobs on paper for an instrument panel and tape to the wall at the front of the plane.

## HOW TO DO IT
• Choose two children to be the pilot and copilot.
• Roleplay the entire plane trip from purchasing tickets, to boarding, to takeoff, to landing.

## VARIATIONS
• The plane can easily become a bus, a train, or a space shuttle.
• Have pillows, magazines, and snack foods and drinks available. Let some children be the flight attendants.
• Say a prayer thanking God for a safe trip and for the fun you have had.

## HOW DID IT GO?
• Did the children get a feeling of what it is really like to take a trip on a plane?
• What were some moments or experiences in which the children sensed awe and wonder at the marvels of God's wonderful world?

# Mother Hen

**MATERIALS NEEDED**

a sheet or a beach towel

*Children will learn how mother hens care for their chicks.*

*Christian Values:* appreciating God's plan for mothers to care for their babies
*Bible:* Luke 13:34 (Jesus cares for people like a mother hen cares for her chicks.)

## GETTING READY
• Prepare an open space for the game.

## HOW TO DO IT
• Explain the game to the children. Say that you are pretending to be a mother hen and they will be your babies. Ask the children to crawl around the room pecking at imaginary seeds or bugs.
• The mother hen (teacher) puts the sheet around her shoulders and flaps her wings as she carefully watches her babies.
• At the appropriate time, sit on a chair and say: "Cluck, cluck, it's getting dark. It's time to gather you in." Gather the chicks and extend your wings around and over them.

## VARIATIONS
• *For older children:* Let one child be a dog or cat who tries to catch the chicks, who then run under the mother hen's wings.

## HOW DID IT GO?
• Did the children enter into the pretend game? Did they sense the mother's watchfulness and care?

## MATERIALS NEEDED

pictures of a variety of
   animals:
     rabbits
     lions or tigers
     fish
     ladybugs
     frogs
     caterpillars
     snakes

# Move Like an Animal

*Children will discover God's plan for animals to move in various ways and will enjoy roleplaying ways animals move.*

*Christian Values:* appreciating God's creatures
*Bible:* Genesis 2:19 (God made many animals and birds.)

## GETTING READY

- Collect pictures of some of the animals and insects listed above.
- Mount pictures on the wall or bulletin board.
- If you use music, check your record player and select appropriate records.

## HOW TO DO IT

- After looking at the pictures, talk about how the animals move from place to place.
- Demonstrate how each animal moves or let the children move like the animal in the picture.
- Say: "Can you hop like a bunny?" "Can you slither like a snake?" "How does a lion move through the forest?"
- Praise God for fun times and for all the ways animals can move.

## VARIATIONS

- Read a book about the animal after the children have experienced the movements.
- Take turns doing the movement, using only a few children at a time.
- Use records to accompany the movements.
- *For older children:* Take a walk to observe animals, birds, and insects.

## HOW DID IT GO?

- Do the children have a better understanding of how animals move from place to place?
- How have you helped children grow in appreciation of all God's creatures?

**MUSIC • LARGE-MUSCLE SKILLS**

# Scarf Butterfly

**MATERIALS NEEDED**

colorful scarves
pipe cleaners

*Children will use their imagination as they enjoy pretending one object is something different.*

**Christian Values:** praising God; developing God's gift of imagination

**Bible:** Genesis 1:27 (God created us with many different gifts.)

## GETTING READY
• Gather scarves for each child.

## HOW TO DO IT
• Talk about how sometimes children pretend one object to be something else. A box can become many things, such as a boat, a train, or a cave.
• Show a scarf and talk about its color and texture. Talk about how it is normally used: to cover the head, to tie as a belt, or to wear with a dress.
• Say: "If we use our imagination, this scarf can be a butterfly." Fold it in half, then in fourths, and tie it in the middle with a pipe cleaner.
• Hold the scarf in the middle and wave it to make a fluttering butterfly.
• Say a prayer thanking God for the gift and fun of imagination.

## VARIATIONS
• Name the butterfly and say: "My friend Lilibeth wants to say hello to all of you." Let the butterfly flutter to each child saying "Hello, (name of child)." Encourage children to respond.
• Make up stories, such as "Lilibeth got caught in the rain and wants to stay in our room. What should we do?"
• Fly the butterfly to appropriate music.

## HOW DID IT GO?
• Did the children feel comfortable doing this imaginative play?

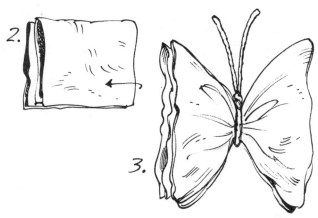

## MATERIALS NEEDED

Each child should bring:
swimsuit
beach towel
sunglasses
beach toys
protective sun lotion
beach bag

# Beach Day

*Children will enjoy pretending to be at the beach on a warm sunny day.*

*Christian Values:* appreciating God's creation of the beach and sea
*Bible:* Acts 4:24 (God created the earth and the sea.)

## GETTING READY
- Plan this activity for the middle of winter to spice up the atmosphere!
- Decorate the room with a large sun and a mural of a beach scene.
- Recruit extra adults to help today.

## HOW TO DO IT
- Tell children they will pretend that they are out in the warm sun.
- Have children put on their swimsuits (over their clothes, if desired).
- Encourage children to stretch out on the towels and bask in the sun.
- Pretend to play in the sand on the beach using their toys.

## VARIATIONS
- Make lemonade to enjoy at the beach.
- Invite another class to join you for a picnic on the beach.
- Bring some sand and a large box. Wet the sand and enjoy making sand sculptures.

## HOW DID IT GO?
- Did younger children need to use more props to help set the mood?
- What moments of spontaneous worship did the children experience?

# Family Barbecue

*Children will explore and appreciate God's plan for families.*

**Christian Values:** appreciating different kinds of families and the togetherness of families
**Bible:** Psalm 133:1 (It is good to be together as a family.)

## MATERIALS NEEDED

shoebox
glue
black strips of paper
cutouts of food to
   barbecue:
   steaks
   corn on the cob
   pork chops

## GETTING READY
- Make a grill by gluing black strips of paper onto the lid of the shoebox.
- Glue pictures of foods on light cardboard.

## HOW TO DO IT
- Talk with the children about things they like to do with their families.
- Ask if anyone has had a family barbecue. Talk about what they did.
- Encourage children to assign family roles. Be sure to vary the types of families!
- Children pretend to arrive at the host family's home. Roleplay what happens next: greet each other, go to patio, drink a cool drink, grill meat, prepare other foods, eat.

## VARIATIONS
- Roleplay other fun times at family events.
- Invite a few parents to participate in the pretending.
- Pretend to go on a trip to visit grandparents: telephone, pack suitcases, load car, prepare food to take, feed pets at home, and so on.

## HOW DID IT GO?
- Can you easily make suggestions and let the children carry out the pretending?
- How well did each child assume responsibility in preparing for the activities?
- Are some children reluctant to pretend? Do they have difficulty in following instructions?

## MATERIALS NEEDED

# Gift Boxes

*Children will develop their skills of imagination by acting out a pretend story.*

*Christian Values:* valuing one another; developing God's gifts of imagination and creativity
*Bible:* 1 John 3:11 (Love one another.)

### GETTING READY
• Arrange a place for a story.

### HOW TO DO IT
• Explain to the children that this is a pretend activity. Say: "I brought a gift box for each of us. The gifts are on the shelves in front of you. Let's take them down." Everyone reaches up and takes the boxes from the pretend shelves.
• Continue the story: "I gave each of you what you really want. Let's open our boxes and see what's inside." Pretend to unwrap the boxes and take out the gifts.
• Pretend to show the children your imaginary gift and tell them what it is.
• Let each child open his or her gift and tell the others about it.

### VARIATIONS
• *For younger children:* Encourage children to imitate your movements. Pretend to look in the box and say: "Susan is eating her apple." Pretend to eat the apple. Or "John got shoes." Everybody puts on shoes.

### HOW DID IT GO?
• How did the children respond to the dramatic play? It is all right if shy ones do not participate. They enjoy the activity by watching.

# My Place

*Children will explore opportunities to relax and enjoy being by themselves.*

**Christian Values:** recognizing uniqueness and value of each person; respecting others
**Bible:** 1 Peter 5:7 (God cares about us.)

## MATERIALS NEEDED

small wading pool
cushions
books, quiet activities
pictures of children
    enjoying quiet activities

## GETTING READY
- Place cushions inside pool, and put in a quiet corner.
- On a wall by the pool hang pictures of children involved with quiet activities.

## HOW TO DO IT
- Show children "My Place" to use during play time.
- Allow one child in "My Place" at one time.
- Make a quiet activity available each day in the area. Change daily.

## VARIATIONS
- If a pool is not available, use a blanket or a sheet.
- Move "My Place" outdoors to a comfortable, shady spot. Help children identify ways to enjoy God's creation outside: look at cloud shapes or tree branches in the breeze.
- Have records of soft familiar music to play while the children are resting or playing quietly.

## HOW DID IT GO?
- Were the quiet activities you selected interesting enough to let the children enjoy their quiet, solitary play long enough to relax?

**SOCIAL-EMOTIONAL RELATIONSHIPS**

## MATERIALS NEEDED

¼-inch hardware cloth
duct or masking tape
blunt yarn needles or
   tapestry needles
several colors of yarn
clear tape (optional)
scissors

# "Needlepoint"

*Children will practice being helpful by sewing.*

*Christian Values:* being helpful; sharing your
   gifts with others
*Bible:* Proverbs 31:13-25 (The woman used her
   sewing skills to make clothes for others.)

## GETTING READY

• Cut the hardware cloth into 6-inch
  squares and bind the edges with tape.
• Thread the needles and tie one end of the
  yarn to a spot on the hardware cloth.

## HOW TO DO IT

• Talk about persons who sew.
• Show the children how to sew the yarn
  up and down through the hardware
  cloth.
• Encourage the children to pretend to sew
  clothes or a blanket for their families.
• Talk about people who need clothing,
  such as the homeless, refugees, the poor.

## VARIATIONS

• *For younger children:* Rather than using a
  needle, tape around the end of a piece of
  yarn and allow the tape to become the
  "needle." Or dip the end of the yarn in
  glue or clear nail polish and let dry.
• Have children bring good used clothing
  to give to an agency that serves the
  needy.

## HOW DID IT GO?

• Did the children show a sense of
  accomplishment in learning a new skill?

# Safety Play

## MATERIALS NEEDED

fabric or ribbon for seat belts
Velcro or other fasteners

*Children will become acquainted with safety procedures for themselves and others.*

**Christian Values:** caring for our bodies; having concern for others' safety
**Bible:** Genesis 1:24-25 (We are to care for all of creation.)

## GETTING READY
- Cut fabric into 3-inch wide strips long enough to fit around back of child-sized chair and around child's waist.
- Attach fasteners to end of fabric strip.

## HOW TO DO IT
- Say the fingerplay "Buckle Up."

### Buckle Up
Here we go, off for a ride, *(motion to come)*
Open the door and climb inside, *(act out)*
Hands in your lap and close the door, *(clap)*
Wait! there's just one job more, *(hold up one finger)*
Hold your seat belt and snap it tight, *(fasten belt)*
Be sure it fits just right, *(shake head yes)*
Start the engine, and we're on our way. *(clap hands)*
We'll stay safely buckled on our ride today.

## VARIATIONS
- *For young children:* Add a car seat in your center to be used in doll play.
- Talk about the importance of wearing seat belts.
- *For older children:* Play a sequence game to put in order the steps of putting on a seat belt. Say the fingerplay and act out the motions.

## HOW DID IT GO?
- Did the children join in the fingerplay motions?
- Could children recall car safety rules?

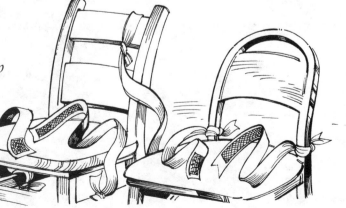

**HEALTH • THINKING SKILLS • LANGUAGE DEVELOPMENT**

# Scrub-a-Dub

**MATERIALS NEEDED**

box (large enough for a
    child to sit in)
bath towels and cloths
various types of brushes
    (toothbrush, hairbrush,
    back or nail brushes)
sponge

*Children will discover that objects have a variety of textures.*

**Christian Values:** becoming aware of God's world; recognizing sense of touch
**Bible:** Genesis 1:26 (God created the world and it was good.)

## GETTING READY
• Prepare the box as a bathtub and have bathing items within easy reach. Place in dramatic play area.

## HOW TO DO IT
• Let a child sit in the bathtub. Discover awareness of textures by asking questions: "Which of these brushes feels soft?" "Which one is hard?"
• Encourage body awareness by asking questions: "What parts of your body could you clean with this?"

## VARIATIONS
• Have texture items with which to compare bath items—smooth fabrics, hard sponge, soap, shampoo.
• Let children play the same game outdoors wearing bathing suits and sitting under a sprinkler shower.

## HOW DID IT GO?
• What kinds of words do the children use to describe textures?
• What body part names did you hear the children mention?

# Sleepover

## MATERIALS NEEDED

Each child should bring one or more of these items from home: pajama top or nightshirt sleeping bag or blanket small pillow

*Children will feel God's love and care as they experience sleeping away from home.*

***Christian Values:*** having fellowship with Christian friends; trusting in God
***Bible:*** Proverbs 17:17 (A friend loves at all times.)

## GETTING READY
- Plan with the children a sleepover day.
- Gather supplies.
- Set up a tent or home area.
- Send home permission forms and a list of supplies to bring.

## HOW TO DO IT
- Discuss times that it may be necessary to spend the night away from home. Talk about fears and concerns about being away from parents.
- Roleplay getting ready: packing, saying good-by, and so on.
- Roleplay arriving, playing a game, or watching TV together.
- Roleplay getting ready for bed: brush teeth, take a bath, and so on. Say a prayer assuring the child of God's love and care.

## VARIATIONS
- This activity can be done as a pretend campout or as a continuation of a pretend airplane or train trip.

## HOW DID IT GO?
- Do you think that children may now feel less apprehensive if they spend the night somewhere other than their home?
- Which children showed symptoms of fear? Discuss this with the parents. What did you do to calm the child?

# Big Box Cave

## MATERIALS NEEDED

large appliance box
paint
cushions
flashlight, books, puzzles
picnic snack food

*Children will have opportunity for solitary or very small group quiet play.*

*Christian Values:* recognizing uniqueness and value of each person; respecting others
*Bible:* 1 John 3:1-2 (We are God's children.)

## GETTING READY

- Cut a large opening in the box or cut out one end.
- Paint outside of box and decorate with bushes or trees.
- Place cushions in corners of cave.
- Add flashlight and quiet activities to cave.

## HOW TO DO IT

- Show children the cave as a center choice for today. Encourage two or three children to play quietly in the cave at one time.
- Let child enjoy reading books with a flashlight inside the cave.
- Eat a picnic lunch with a friend inside the cave.

## VARIATIONS

- Use the cave as a quiet corner for listening to tapes of stories. A child can act out a story by placing figures on the flannelboard.
- Encourage an adult to snuggle with a pair of two-year-olds to read a story, sing a song, or talk about children's interests.
- Use a portable radio or record player for listening.

## HOW DID IT GO?

- How many children were able to play constructively in the cave without conflict?
- Did children understand the concept of a quiet play space?

**SOCIAL-EMOTIONAL RELATIONSHIPS**

# Changing Seasons

*Children will become aware of the world around them in different seasons.*

*Christian Values:* appreciating God's plan for seasonal changes in some places
*Bible:* Genesis 1:14 (God created four seasons.)

## MATERIALS NEEDED

pictures of various seasons
records or tapes of sounds or music for creative movement

## GETTING READY
- Use this activity during each season.
- Make a seasonal bulletin board or hang pictures to show seasonal changes.
- Select appropriate music.

## HOW TO DO IT
- Discuss the current season and things we can see or sounds we hear.
- Encourage children to pretend to be or to do some of these things.
- *Winter:* pretend to be a snowman, snowflakes falling softly to the ground, wind whistling in bare trees, animals sleeping in hibernation.
- *Fall:* pretend to be falling leaves, squirrels gathering nuts, raking leaves, wind blowing leaves, and so on.
- Pray spontaneous prayers of thanks for special moments of beauty and awe during each season.

## VARIATIONS
- Take a walk with the children to observe seasonal changes. Collect fall leaves, watch an ant build a home, and pick wild flowers.
- Encourage individual children to create their own pretend situations and demonstrate for the class. Then let all children follow the leader.

## HOW DID IT GO?
- Was there other preparation that could have been made to help the children understand some of the seasonal changes?

# Tent Play

## MATERIALS NEEDED

tables
sheer curtains
cushions
dolls and accessories
cooking and cleaning
  items

*Children will find satisfaction in using their imaginations in group play.*

*Christian Values:* helping others; becoming aware of community and working together
*Bible:* Hebrews 13:16 (Help one another.)

## GETTING READY

- Make a tent in an area of the room with plenty of space for moving around. Place two tables together and drape fabric over them.
- Gather supplies from the family living center to place in the tent.

## HOW TO DO IT

- Act out a Bible story about how to welcome visitors and live as neighbors.
- Give suggestions to get play started: "Two children could live in this house and two in that house." "Invite your neighbors to visit you."
- Children may play dress-up, cook meals, care for a baby, tend the garden, or do other daily work.
- Invite an older person to tell stories around the campfire outside the tent at night.

## VARIATIONS

- Make tents by draping fabric over large hoops suspended from the ceiling.
- Make and bake bread in an "outdoor" oven. Say or sing a prayer of thanks.

## HOW DID IT GO?

- Did the children find play in a quiet, cozy tent satisfying?
- How many children were able to play cooperatively?

**LANGUAGE DEVELOPMENT**

# Weather Game

## MATERIALS NEEDED

old magazines
scissors

*Children will begin to understand God's plan for weather by dramatizing what they would do in various situations.*

*Christian Values:* respecting God's creation;
    developing thinking skills
*Bible:* Psalm 135:6-7 (God's plan for creation
    includes different kinds of weather.)

## GETTING READY
• Cut out pictures of clothes worn in different seasons and weather.

## HOW TO DO IT
• Show some pictures of different kinds of weather. Talk about ways the children are dressed.
• Say that some weather conditions are frightening but others are enjoyable. Let the children share some of their feelings and experiences.
• Ask the children to dramatize certain weather-related situations such as
    walking in the rain
    walking through deep snow
    sliding on ice
    walking barefoot on a hot sidewalk
    what they do in a thunderstorm

## VARIATIONS
• Ask children to pick out different clothing for various kinds of weather.

## HOW DID IT GO?
• How comfortable were the children in roleplaying? It takes time for most children to overcome fear, so give opportunity for informal dramatics.
• Did the children express their feelings? What feelings did they share? Were they appropriate for the situation?

**LANGUAGE DEVELOPMENT • SCIENCE DEVELOPMENT**

# Make Car Repairs

*Children will learn to be helpful to others by pretending to make car repairs.*

*Christian Values:* being helpful; choosing a vocation
*Bible:* 1 Corinthians 4:12a (We work with our hands.)

## MATERIALS NEEDED

toy cars and trucks
toy wrenches and tools
tire pump
tool box
sponges and water
car wax
large wooden blocks
piece of garden hose

## GETTING READY

- Set up the mechanic's shop where it will have plenty of room but be out of the way of other activities.
- Use a tall box and a piece of garden hose to make a gas pump.

## HOW TO DO IT

- Talk with the children about taking turns and about using the tools and parts carefully.
- Let the children pretend to use the tools to change a tire, repair the lights, charge the battery, pour in oil, and so on.
- Encourage both girls and boys to participate and to put away toys when finished.

## VARIATIONS

- *For younger children:* Provide fewer tools and pretend to repair large toy cars and trucks.
- Let the children wash and wax the wooden cars and trucks.
- Fill the cars and trucks with gas.

## HOW DID IT GO?

- How did the children play imaginatively?
- Did the children seem to understand the importance of repairing cars for others?

**SOCIAL-EMOTIONAL RELATIONSHIPS • THINKING SKILLS**

# Fishing Game

Children will learn that God created fish to give us food and enjoyment.

**Christian Values:** finding appreciation for God's gift of fish; taking turns
**Bible:** Matthew 4:18 (Fishing was an important vocation in biblical times.)

## MATERIALS NEEDED

large sheet of blue posterboard
construction paper
glue
sticks for fishing poles
30-inch pieces of string
magnets
paper clips
frying pan
small pictures of objects beginning with certain consonant sounds

## GETTING READY

- Cut a pond from the posterboard. Cut fish from construction paper and insert a paper clip on the mouth.
- Attach a magnet to a piece of string and tie to a stick.
- Cut out pictures beginning with *D* and glue to one side of the fish. Add a few pictures beginning with other letters. Spread pictures face down in the pond.

## HOW TO DO IT

- Let a few children fish from the pond. When a fish is caught, the child tells what letter the picture begins with and its sound.
- If the picture begins with *D*, the child puts the fish in the frying pan. If the sound is not *D*, the fish is thrown back and the child fishes again.

## VARIATIONS

- *For older children:* Fish for letters of the alphabet or numbers. When a fish is caught, name the letter or numeral.

## HOW DID IT GO?

- Could the children identify the letter sounds?
- Did the children wait patiently for their turn?
- What evidence was there to show children grew in awe and wonder of God's creation?

**LANGUAGE DEVELOPMENT**

# Moving Day

## MATERIALS NEEDED

boxes
small suitcases
toy wagons or carts
old newspapers

*Children will discover how to work together to move.*

*Christian Values:* knowing families work together; knowing God is always with us
*Bible:* Ruth 1:1-19 (Naomi and her family moved.)

## GETTING READY
• Plan how you can move the family living area to a new location in the room.
• Have extra adult help today.

## HOW TO DO IT
• Children can pack the family living center and move it to its new location. Decide how to take dishes, toys, and so on.
• Rearrange and set up the new center.
• Talk with the children about how it feels to live in a new place. Help children remember that God is always with us wherever we are. Sing "Prayer Song."

## VARIATIONS
• Follow up the experience with an appropriate story about a child moving.
• Use this activity if you have a child moving or a new child who has just moved and is in your class.
• Encourage children to talk about times they have moved. How did they feel? Talk about different reasons for moving.

## HOW DID IT GO?
• Did the children work together to make the move?
• Did they like the change?

### Prayer Song

God is al - ways near me. God will al - ways hear me when I pray. _____

WORDS and MUSIC: Elizabeth Parker • © 1975 by Graded Press

**SOCIAL-EMOTIONAL RELATIONSHIPS**

# Be a Painter

Children will discover a community worker and how people work together.

**Christian Values:** working together; using our talents

**Bible:** Romans 12:4-7 (God has given us different gifts that can be used to help people.)

### MATERIALS NEEDED

paint brushes (2 to 3 inches wide)
boxes
plastic pails
water and cloths
cleaning brushes

## GETTING READY
- Determine what outside area the children will water-paint: sidewalk, wall, side of a building, fence, equipment.
- Have pails of water and other equipment ready in a safe place outside.
- Have children wear play clothes.

## HOW TO DO IT
- Talk about the tools a painter needs and the jobs done: scraping paint, sanding, painting, cleaning up.
- Go outside. Show the children where they can work. Guide the children in deciding which job each one will do. Talk about cooperating and working together.

## VARIATIONS
- Have a Water Day Celebration and use this activity as well as other forms of water play.
- *For older children:* emphasize the contributions a painter makes to a community.

## HOW DID IT GO?
- Did the children enjoy the water play?
- Did they view the painter as a community helper?
- Did the children grow in their ability to play together and cooperate with each other?

**SOCIAL STUDIES READINESS · LARGE-MUSCLE SKILLS**

## MATERIALS NEEDED

red and orange felt
light cardboard
brown and green
  construction paper
white yarn
cash register
toy money
scissors

# Be a Pizza Cook

*Children will become aware of and grow in appreciation of persons who help us have food.*

*Christian Values:* thanking God for people who help us; developing God's gift of learning
*Bible:* Genesis 1:26-28 (God created us with the ability to think.)

## GETTING READY

- Cut a circle from cardboard for the pizza crust, a slightly smaller red felt circle for pizza sauce, and smaller orange circles for pepperoni.
- Let children cut green snips for green peppers, bite-size pieces of brown for mushrooms, and one-inch pieces of white yarn for cheese.

## HOW TO DO IT

- Set up the pizza parlor in the housekeeping area and set the different ingredients in separate containers.
- Let the children take turns being waiters, pizza cooks, and customers.
- Decide early how many customers each team of workers can serve at a time so that waiting time is minimized

## VARIATIONS

- *For younger children:* Invite a parent to make real pizzas with the class.
- *For older children:* Plan a field trip to a pizza parlor. See page 218.

## HOW DID IT GO?

- Did everybody have a turn with the activity today? What arrangement will you make so the ones who didn't have a turn today can have an opportunity tomorrow or another day?
- What suggestions did the children make in running the pizza store?

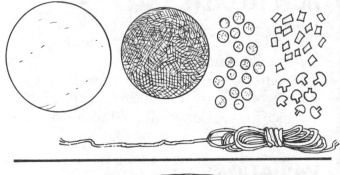

# Sailing Boats

Children will discover that one means of travel is by boat.

**Christian Values:** using God's creation for good; developing our talents

**Bible:** Matthew 14:22 (Travel by boat was common in Jesus' day.)

### MATERIALS NEEDED

large boxes to sit in
one yardstick for each box
tagboard or posterboard
scissors and knife
wide masking tape
tempera paint and brushes
one large blue bed sheet

## GETTING READY

- Cut triangle-shaped sails out of the posterboard. Cut two horizontal slits in the sail and insert a yardstick. Tape securely.
- Tape a yardstick to the inside of each box.
- Place the sheet on the floor for a pretend ocean.

## HOW TO DO IT

- Tell one of the Bible stories about Jesus, Paul, or the disciples traveling by boat.
- Let children paint the outside of the boxes and let them dry.
- Children sit in the boats and are ready to pretend to sail. If the box is large, place small chairs or a bench inside it.

## VARIATIONS

- *For younger children:* Let children sail small plastic boats in a dishpan of water.
- *For older children:* Celebrate Columbus Day by using three ships called Niña, Pinta, and Santa Maria to tell the story of Columbus.
- Use paper-towel tubes taped together for spy glasses.

## HOW DID IT GO?

- In which units can you use this activity?
- In what ways was it effective?

## MATERIALS NEEDED

old shoes
small hammer
small paper bags
shelves for display
toy cash register
toy money
cobbler's apron

# Shoe Repair Shop

*Children will discover one way people help each other when they pretend to work in a shoe repair shop.*

**Christian Values:** appreciating people who help us; thanking God for people who help us
**Bible:** 1 Corinthians 4:12a (We work with our hands.)

## GETTING READY
• Arrange the shoe repair shop away from most other activities.

## HOW TO DO IT
• Let the children take turns pretending to repair shoes and being a customer. Caution children about using the hammer.
• Encourage both boys and girls to be shoe repairers.
• Talk about how the shoe repair person helps others. Say a prayer of thanks for people who use God's gifts to help others.
• Have the repair shop available for a few days.

## VARIATIONS
• *For younger children:* Provide toy hammers to use in repairing shoes.
• Have extra shoelaces so children can practice lacing or tying their shoes.
• *For older children:* Have old shoes and soft rags so children can shine shoes using clear wax polish.

## HOW DID IT GO?
• In what ways did the children enter into the roleplaying?
• How did they show appreciation for the help cobblers give to people?

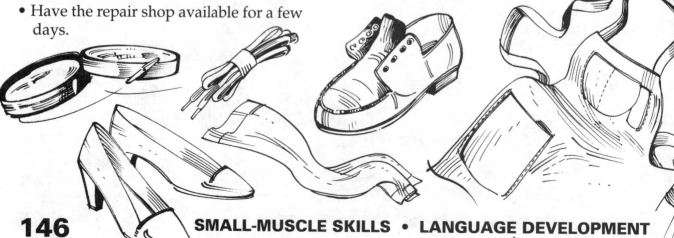

# Body Parts

*Children will name their body parts and praise God with music.*

*Christian Values:* enhancing self-esteem; responding to God with gratitude
*Bible:* Psalm 34:1 (I will always thank God.)

## MATERIALS NEEDED

music with distinct beat and rhythm
record player

## GETTING READY
- Decide what space you will use for the activity.

## HOW TO DO IT
- Talk about the body parts and how good it is that God gave us good bodies.
- Play the music. Have the children repeat the names of the body parts and imitate your movements such as
    *heel, heel* (touch floor with heels alternately)
    *feet, feet* (slide feet to side)
    *fingers, fingers* (touch thumb with the rest of your fingers).
- Name as many body parts as you want, and make up your own movements.
- Thank God for our good bodies.

## VARIATIONS
- *For younger children:* Use a chant:
    **Teacher**: I'll touch my nose.
    **Children**: I'll touch my nose.
    **Teacher**: I'll touch my mouth.
        And so on.
- *For older children:* Use a record of jazz or rock music with no voices. Then chant the phrase to the music as you name each of the body parts:
    *I'll touch my face* (rest a phrase or clap hands)
    *I'll touch my nose* (rest a phrase)
    *I'll touch my ears,* and so on.

## HOW DID IT GO?
- Which of the two-year-olds can name their major body parts?
- Did the children try to make up their own movements?

# Clap a Song

## MATERIALS NEEDED

music records from
 Sunday school curricula
record player

*Children will learn to praise God by singing and clapping to music.*

*Christian Values:* using senses to praise God; remembering our Christian heritage
*Bible:* Psalm 47:1 (Clap your hands; shout to God with loud songs of joy.)

## GETTING READY
• Gather some familiar songs from the children's Sunday school records.

## HOW TO DO IT
• Let the children choose songs they would like to sing. Make suggestions from the records you have.
• Play the song through once. Then try out a variety of ways to clap with the song: clap the rhythm, clap the words.
• Say a prayer of thanks to God for good times. Encourage children to name things for which they are thankful.

## VARIATIONS
• *For older children:* Use a combination of clapping, slapping knees, and touching the floor.

## HOW DID IT GO?
• Was it harder for some children than others to clap to the music? How can you help children improve coordination?
• Does music and clapping make everyone feel good?

# Pass the Present

*Children will affirm and thank God for their growth.*

*Christian Values:* enhancing self-esteem; praising God for growth

*Bible:* Luke 2:40 (Children grow today as Jesus grew.)

## MATERIALS NEEDED

a shoebox
birthday wrapping paper
stickers or tape
record with "Happy Birthday" song or instrumental music

## GETTING READY
- Place stickers in box. Wrap box and lid separately so box can open.
- Have a birthday list for 5- and 6-year-olds.

## HOW TO DO IT
- Explain how to play the game.
- When the music starts, children pass the gift box around the circle until the teacher stops the music.
- The child holding the box responds by giving his or her age and birthday.
- When a child answers correctly, the child can select a sticker to wear.
- Start the music and begin the game again.

## VARIATIONS
- Children enjoy opening presents. Wrap a box in colored tissue paper and use this game to reinforce other ideas.

- Children will cut out pictures of objects and paste onto the gift boxes according to the theme. For example: I am thankful for _____. I can show love when I _____. I can help by _____.
- Say a thank-you prayer for God's plan for growth.

## HOW DID IT GO?
- Were the children able to give an appropriate response?
- In what ways did the children show they enjoyed the game?

# Yes, I Can

## MATERIALS NEEDED

space for children to move about
record player, record from the 1985 Age 2 Sunday school curriculum song "Yes, I Can"

*Children will grow in their ability to follow directions as they sing and move with music.*

**Christian Values:** praising God with our body movements; using God's gift of creativity
**Bible:** Psalm 150:3-6 (Praise God with instruments and dance.)

## GETTING READY
- Play the song to become familiar with it. Practice singing it.
- Prepare an area for movement.

## HOW TO DO IT
- Encourage the children to talk about things they can do now that they could not do when they were younger.
- Remind the children of God's plan for growth and how they can do new and harder things as they grow. Pray a prayer of thanksgiving to God.
- Let children practice singing the song before attempting to do the movements.
- Talk about the actions; then have children move as the song directs.

## VARIATIONS
- Let children think of new things they can do and create more verses and movements to go with the song.

## HOW DID IT GO?
- Did children enjoy moving to the music?
- Could children remember the movements to do?
- How well could children remember things they could do when they were younger?

# Creation Parade

*Children will express thanksgiving for creation by having a parade.*

**Christian Values:** expressing thanks to God; awareness of creation

**Bible:** Psalm 19:1 (The heavens are telling the wonders of God's great creation.)

## MATERIALS NEEDED

song tune: "He's Got the Whole World in His Hands"
record player
musical instruments
teaching pictures of nature

## GETTING READY
- Display pictures of nature from previous units. Bring objects of nature to create a display.
- Practice singing the song.
- Gather music instruments.

## HOW TO DO IT
- Play the song and sing along, using these words:
  "God made the whole world, let's praise God (clap) (repeat line 3 times)
  "God made the whole big wonderful world."
- Let children observe with their senses the objects in the display. Watch for moments of awe and wonder where spontaneous worship is a possibility.
- Praise God for the wonderful world by having a parade while playing the rhythm instruments and singing.

## VARIATIONS
- Invite someone who can play the piano, guitar, or electronic keyboard to play the song.
- Take a walk outdoors and sit beneath a tree or encourage children to go outside at night to observe the heavens.

## HOW DID IT GO?
- Did most of the children participate?
- At what points did the children respond to the wonders of God's creation?

## MATERIALS NEEDED

song "Rocking"
record, if available
record player

# Act Out the Song "Rocking"

*Children will sing with friends and act out the song cooperatively.*

**Christian Values:** working together; being kind to friends
**Bible:** 1 Corinthians 3:9 (We are workers with God.)

## GETTING READY
• Practice singing the song "Rocking."

## HOW TO DO IT
• Use this song in a unit on fishermen. Talk about the different kinds of boats used for travel.
• Introduce the song "Rocking."
• Have children sit in pairs on the floor facing each other holding hands, bottoms of feet firmly together. As they sing, children pull gently back and forth.
• As you sing the second stanza, have children stand and pretend to fish.

## VARIATIONS
• Add stanzas and motions for other kinds of boats. Sing the song again as children put hands over head to form a triangular sail.
• As you sing stanza 2, children form a circle, reach out and hold the net, and pull together hard to bring the heavy load of fish into the boat.

## HOW DID IT GO?
• Did all the children participate in the actions?
• Could the children think of additional stanzas to use?

### Rocking

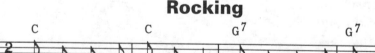

1. Rock-ing, rock-ing in our boat; Rock-ing, rock-ing in our boat;

2. Fishing, fishing in our boat
3. Sailing, sailing in our boat
4. Rocking, rocking in our boat

Rock-ing, rock-ing in our boat; Rock-ing in our boat.

WORDS: Evelyn M. Andre • MUSIC: V. Earle Copes •. © 1960 by Graded Press

# Scarf/Streamer Dancing

*Children will praise and thank God by moving to music with scarves or streamers.*

**Christian Values:** praising God; becoming aware of God's presence

**Bible:** Psalm 150:3-6 (Praise God with instruments and dance.)

## MATERIALS NEEDED

record player or tape player
instrumental music that expresses feelings
nylon scarves or crepe-paper streamers

## GETTING READY
- Select appropriate music.
- Have the materials handy.
- Clear an area large enough for the children to move around.

## HOW TO DO IT
- Talk with the children about enjoyable things they have done today.
- Say: "Creative movement is one way we can thank God." Ask the children to listen to the music and respond with their bodies and their scarves or streamers.
- Encourage the children to talk about how they felt.

## VARIATIONS
- The children's responses will vary with their age.
- Use scarves seasonally as you pretend to be leaves falling or new plants growing.
- Pretend to be animals, birds, or insects.

## HOW DID IT GO?
- Did the children seem free to respond to the music or did they look to you for direction?

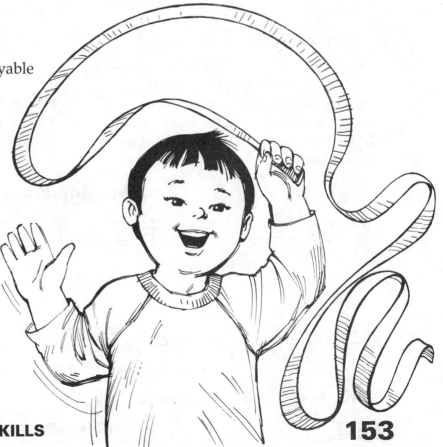

**MUSIC • LARGE-MUSCLE SKILLS**

# Swinging Song

## MATERIALS NEEDED

"Swinging Song"
record of 2/4 music

*Children will experience praising God together by playing a musical game.*

*Christian Values:* enjoying friendship; praising God through music
*Bible:* Psalm 34:3 (Let us praise God together.)

## GETTING READY

• Clear safe area for movement. If limits are needed, put a piece of masking tape on the floor for each pair or mark the space with chalk.

## HOW TO DO IT

• Divide children in pairs and help them face their partner and hold hands.
• Practice moving to the music on the record or as they hum the tune.
• Talk about things for which they want to praise God.

## VARIATIONS

• *For older children:* Emphasize movements of high and low, fast and slow, or other opposites. Older children can match their swinging to the speed of the music.
• Let children on the inside circle move to the right one person. New friends may give new meanings to the act of praise.

## HOW DID IT GO?

• Were children able to cooperate with another child in doing the movements?

### Swinging Song

Swing - ing, swing - ing, Swing - ing up to the sky!

Swing - ing, swing - ing, Swing - ing down to the ground.

WORDS and MUSIC: Nancy Coghill • © 1992 by Cokesbury

# Ankle Bell Dance

*Children will express joy and celebration through dance.*

*Christian Values:* affirming uniqueness of self and others; gaining a sense of God's community
*Bible:* Ephesians 2:19 (We are all members of the family of God.)

## MATERIALS NEEDED

shoelaces
jingle bells
music record or tape
drums

## GETTING READY
• String three jingle bells onto each shoelace, tying a knot between each bell. Knot each end of the lace to prevent bells from slipping off.

## HOW TO DO IT
• Tie bells to the children's ankles.
• Encourage children to think of some happy times they remember. Say: "We can thank God by dancing to happy music." Play traditional Native American music, if available.
• Let some children take turns beating the drums as others dance creatively.

## VARIATIONS
• Tie bells on wrists or upper arms to encourage arm movement while standing or sitting.
• Introduce other Native American traditional celebration rituals and talk about modern celebrations.

## HOW DID IT GO?
• Were children comfortable moving in the unstructured dance?
• Were the bells helpful in encouraging more movement by the children? Did children enjoy experimenting with the sounds?

# Butterflies

## MATERIALS NEEDED

butterflies (see pages 19, 41, 127)
filmy scarves (2 per child)
pictures or books about butterflies

*Children will grow in appreciation of butterflies as they respond to a song with creative movement.*

*Christian Values:* appreciating God's gift of butterflies; developing creativity
*Bible:* Psalm 150:3-6 (Praise God with dance.)

## GETTING READY
• Learn to sing the song "Butterflies."
• Increase your knowledge of butterflies.

## HOW TO DO IT
• Show pictures of butterflies. Encourage children to talk about butterflies.
• Practice singing the song "Butterflies."
• Let each child select two filmy scarves to be their wings, or use one of the butterflies made earlier. Hold arms out as they sing, and move the arms up and down to the rhythm of the music.
• Thank God for the beauty of butterflies.

## VARIATIONS
• Take a field trip to observe butterflies.
• Call your library to see if they have videos about butterflies that you could borrow to show the children.
• Go outside with your tape recorder and let the children fly like butterflies!

## HOW DID IT GO?
• What evidence did you have that children grew in awareness of God's wonderful world?
• In what ways did the children respond creatively to the rhythm of the music?

### Butterflies

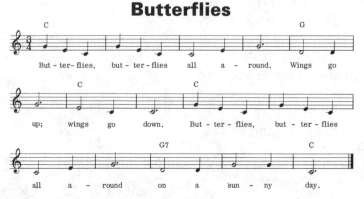

WORDS and MUSIC: Elaine Lockwood • © 1974 by Graded Press

# Bamboo Plate Dance

*Children will learn about people of other cultures by doing a Filipino dance.*

**Christian Values:** valuing others; using God's gift of creativity
**Bible:** Acts 10:34 (God loves and accepts all people.)

## MATERIALS NEEDED

bamboo plate holders (colorful plastic plates could also be used)
waltz music
record player or tape recorder
use the Filipino song "My Nipa Hut," if available

## GETTING READY
- Use in a unit on multiethnic cultures.
- Check mission study materials for 1989–90 for "My Nipa Hut."

## HOW TO DO IT
- Play the waltz music. Let children count 1-2-3, 1-2-3, clapping on the first beat.
- Give each child a bamboo plate. Tell the children to hold the plate at waist level in front of them with both hands.
- Then do the following movements in rhythm.
  1. Hold plate out at arms length on count 1, hold in place for count 2, back to position on count 3.
  2. Move plate to left side on count 1, hold in place for count 2, back to position on count 3. Repeat to right side.

## VARIATIONS
- Encourage older children to add other movements:

1. Raise hands and swing from side to side.
2. Stand and while swaying raised hands from side to side, make one step in the same direction as the hands.
3. Step back to original position and repeat.

## HOW DID IT GO?
- How did children respond to the difficulty of the activity?

 1.

 2.

 3.

 4.

## MATERIALS NEEDED

music that has a strong 4/4
   beat
record player or tape
   player
wide-brimmed straw hat
masking tape

# Circle Dancing

*Children will enjoy being creative with the music.*

*Christian Values:* enhancing self-esteem; being
   grateful to God
*Bible:* Psalm 34:1 (I will always thank God.)

## GETTING READY

- Make a large circle on the floor with masking tape or chalk.
- Listen to the music and practice the movements.

## HOW TO DO IT

- Have teachers and children march around in a circle and hold hands.
- Play the music and have the children do what you do as a teacher calls:
    Slide to the right,
        one, two, three, four.
    Slide to the left,
        one, two, three, four.
    Walk to the center and raise your
        hands.
    Swing them to the left,
        and swing them to the right
        (and so on).

## VARIATIONS

- *For older children:* Do the Mexican Hat Dance. Put a large straw hat in the middle of the circle. Let the children dance around the hat to some Spanish music. Use simple steps at the level your children feel capable.

## HOW DID IT GO?

- How freely did the children respond to the music?
- How did you affirm all the children's efforts? Do you have any children with handicapping conditions that need special consideration?

# Having Fun Today

*Children will have fun doing a circle dance together.*

*Christian Values:* appreciating God's gifts of music and friends
*Bible:* Psalm 75:1 (We give thanks to you, O God.)

## MATERIALS NEEDED

record player
song "Having Fun Today"
  from 1991 Age 2
  Summer curriculum

## GETTING READY
- Clear a space large enough for the children to form a circle.
- Learn to sing the song and be familiar with the movements.

## HOW TO DO IT
- Play the song "Having Fun Today" and practice singing it until children are familiar with the tune and words.
- Talk about the fun of doing things together with friends. Follow the directions in the song and enjoy doing the motions.
- Thank God for good times at school through music.

## VARIATIONS
- *For younger children:* Vary the movements to more simple ones.
- *For older children:* Try several small groups instead of one large group of children.

## HOW DID IT GO?
- Do the children enjoy participating in group activities with their friends?
- Were they able to listen and follow the directions given in the song?

## MATERIALS NEEDED

instrumental record or
tape
large sheets of blue
construction paper
scissors

# Musical Puddles

*Children will enjoy playing a noncompetitive musical game.*

*Christian Values:* reaching out to others;
cooperating
*Bible:* Ephesians 4:32 (Be kind to one another.)

## GETTING READY

- Cut puddle shapes out of blue paper. Have one less puddle than children.
- Arrange the puddles on the floor in random order.
- Place a record on the player.

## HOW TO DO IT

- Children will stand in a circle around the puddles.
- The leader starts the music and children walk around the circle.
- When the music stops, children quickly step on a puddle, but one child is left out.
- Say: "Erin needs a friend. Who will share a puddle?" After sharing occurs, everyone holds hands and makes the circle again.
- Avoid competition by not removing puddles, so all children can play again.

## VARIATIONS

- Use the same game technique with other shapes to fit your theme. For example: winter—snowflake, valentines—heart, Christmas—trees.

## HOW DID IT GO?

- Did the children respond well to everyone being included?
- What evidence did you see that the children made friends?

# Play Londonbashi

*Children will grow in appreciation of other cultures by playing a familiar game in another language.*

*Christian Values:* valuing all people as God's children; playing together

*Bible:* Mark 12:31 (Love your neighbor as yourself.)

## MATERIALS NEEDED

song "Londonbashi"

## GETTING READY
- Practice singing the song.
- Clear an area to play the game.

## HOW TO DO IT
- Sing "London Bridge" in English first. Then sing by phrases in Japanese.
- Play the game singing in Japanese. Two children join both hands and hold arms high to form a bridge. Other children form a line and march around and under the bridge. When the last word is sung, the bridge children lower their arms and try to capture a player.

## VARIATIONS
- *For younger children:* Sing only in the English language and play the game.
- Invite a Japanese friend in to sing the song and to teach other games.
- *For older children:* Invite children from other cultures to sing the song in their own language.

## HOW DID IT GO?
- Did the unfamiliar language add new excitement to a very familiar game?
- Are there other Japanese words or songs the children could learn?

### Londonbashi

WORDS and MUSIC: Traditional • TRANSLATION: Masahiro Kasama • Translation © 1992 by Cokesbury

## MATERIALS NEEDED

masking tape
pictures of quiet situations
music record or tape

# Tiptoe, Shhh!

*Children will become sensitive to their impact on other people and the world around them.*

*Christian Values:* developing self-control; respecting creation
*Bible:* Job 37:14 (Consider the wonderful works of God.)

## GETTING READY
- Make a trail on the floor by using masking tape to wind around tables and chairs.
- Display pictures of quiet things along the trail: puppies sleeping, deer eating, bunny in the grass, and so on.

## HOW TO DO IT
- Invite several children to tiptoe around the trail.
- When they come to a picture, they say, "Shhh," and all stop.
- Ask one child to whisper to the others what is happening in the picture.
- Tiptoe to the next picture.

## VARIATIONS
- *For younger children:* Twos may be able to name some of the objects in the pictures and will need more teacher guidance.
- *For older children:* Use some pictures that show some quiet and some noisy activities. Let children choose an appropriate response to each picture by walking past active scenes and tiptoeing past quiet scenes.

## HOW DID IT GO?
- How much control did children have over the volume of their voices?
- What was the listening response to whispering?

# A Friend Loves

## MATERIALS NEEDED

song "A Friend Loves"
record of song from 1985
Age 2 curriculum
pictures of loving friends
from around the world

*Children around the world have friends and like to sing songs.*

*Christian Values:* appreciating all of God's people; enhancing self-esteem
*Bible:* 1 John 3:1-2 (We are all children of God.)

## GETTING READY
- Learn to sing the song.
- Display pictures of friends from around the world.

## HOW TO DO IT
- Let children look at the pictures of friends and talk about what they are doing.
- Talk about how people in other countries are just like we are. They need friends and have friends too.
- Introduce the song; play it on the record player (if possible).

## VARIATIONS
- Ask a Japanese friend or a Hispanic friend to visit the class and sing the song.
- If you have children in your school who speak another language, invite them to sing the song as they would in their own language.

## HOW DID IT GO?
- Did the children enjoy singing a song in a different language?
- Did children grow in their appreciation of children in other countries?

## A Friend Loves

| | English: | A | friend | loves | at | all | times, | A | friend | loves | at | all | times. |
| | Japanese: | To | mo - da | chi | wa | ai - su - ru, | | To | mo - da | chi | wa | ai - su - ru. |
| | Spanish: | Te | a - mo | por | siem - pre, | | | Te | a - mo | por | siem - pre. |

WORDS: Proverbs 17:17 • MUSIC: Philip R. Dietterich • Music © 1965 by Graded Press

# Beach Fun

### MATERIALS NEEDED

song "A Beach Song"

*Children will praise God by expressing themselves creatively through movement.*

**Christian Values:** sensing the wonder of God's creation; developing God's gift of creativity
**Bible:** 1 Timothy 4:4 (Everything that God created is good.)

## GETTING READY
- Learn the song; feel the rhythm.
- Practice ways of moving to the music. Use balloons, scarves, and so on.

## HOW TO DO IT
- Sing the song with children. Teachers may need to demonstrate creative movements for the children.
- Let children move individually to their own creative movements. Call out ideas (the waves are rolling in higher) related to the beach to help the children.

## VARIATIONS
- Let children dramatize the song using simple props:
  "drive" to the beach with a steering wheel;
  toss a beach ball with a partner;
  dig in pretend sand with shovel and bucket.

## HOW DID IT GO?
- Do the children seem comfortable in assuming leadership roles and suggesting ideas for movement?

### A Beach Song

1. Driv-ing to the beach, we're driv-ing, driv-ing. Driv-ing to the beach, now here __ we go!
2. Dig-ging in the sand, we're dig-ging, dig-ging. Dig-ging in the sand, now here __ we go!

3. Jumping in the waves, we're jumping, jumping. Jumping in the waves, now here we go!
4. Playing with our beach ball, playing, playing. Playing with our beach ball, here we go.

WORDS and MUSIC: Nancy Coghill • © 1992 by Cokesbury

# Echo Songs

*Children will praise God through music as both leaders and followers.*

**Christian Values:** appreciating ideas and talents of each person; praising God with music

**Bible:** Psalm 84:4 (Happy are those who come to church and sing God's praise.)

**MATERIALS NEEDED**

songs familiar to the children ("Do You Know?" "God Loves," "God Is So Good," "Prayer Song" "Thank You, God" from *Sing and Be Joyful* songbook, pages 86, 88, 92, 97) record player or cassette

## GETTING READY
- Identify several familiar songs with short phrases that can be sung in echo style.
- Check usability of equipment.

## HOW TO DO IT
- Sing or play the song to the children.
- Explain that you will now take turns singing the song with them by letting them echo what you sing.
- Sing first phrase, *they sing*; sing second phrase, *they sing*; and so on.

## VARIATIONS
- *For younger children:* Use a puppet to help young children know when it is their turn to sing. Hold the puppet behind you and bring it to the front to "help" the children sing.
- *For older children:* Let the children select songs they enjoy. Let one child lead and the teacher and class echo.
- Make up a praise song as a group. Sing in the echo style.

## HOW DID IT GO?
- Was it difficult for the children to wait for their turn to echo?
- Were songs with motions easier to echo? To sing?

# I Am First

## MATERIALS NEEDED

record player
marching music of short
duration

*Children will learn concern for others by taking turns being leader as they play a musical game.*

*Christian Values:* appreciating and valuing others; enjoying God's gift of music
*Bible:* Mark 10:31 (Sometimes we will go first, other times we will go last.)

## GETTING READY
- Move some of your equipment to give you more room to move.

## HOW TO DO IT
- Explain how the game is to be played.
- Talk about what it means to be first and why it is important for others to be leader sometimes. Relate the experiences to feelings children have.
- Line the children up. The first child is the leader as they march around the room. When the music stops (either automatically or by the teacher), the last child in the line comes to the front and becomes the leader.
- Continue playing until every child has a chance to be the leader.

## VARIATIONS
- Children can use musical instruments as they march around the room.
- *For older children:* Older children may skip, skate, or gallop.
- Go to the library and find a good book on cooperative games to lessen children's competitiveness.

## HOW DID IT GO?
- How did the children respond to the idea of being first and last?
- Which children need more encouragement in taking turns?

# Welcome, Friend

*Children will learn one way to make a friendly response to other children by playing a game.*

**Christian Values:** showing kindness; having a sense of community
**Bible:** Ephesians 2:19 (We are all God's children.)

**MATERIALS NEEDED**

song "Welcome, Friend"

## GETTING READY

• Learn to sing the song or have a person record it on tape.

## HOW TO DO IT

• Have a teacher walk around a small circle of children and sing "Welcome, Friend."
• As each name is sung, that child joins hands with the teacher and they continue going around in the circle.
• Continue singing until all children are part of the circle and playing the game.

## VARIATIONS

• *For older children:* Play outdoors and welcome another class of friends into the circle as you sing.

## HOW DID IT GO?

• How difficult was it for children to wait for their name to be sung?
• Did they feel comfortable in the large circle?

### Welcome, Friend

1. Wel - come, friend, come walk with me. Wel - come, friend, come walk with me.
2. Eve - ry - bod - y clap your hands, clap your hands, yes clap your hands.

Wel - come, friend, come walk with me, }
Eve - ry - bod - y clap your hands. } walk a - round the cir - cle.

*Other possible stanzas:* Welcome, (insert child's name), come walk with me
Everybody stomp your feet
Everybody bend your knees
Everybody stretch up tall
Everybody march along

WORDS and MUSIC: Nancy Coghill • © 1992 by Cokesbury

# Rainbow Song

## MATERIALS NEEDED

pieces of construction
   paper in red, yellow,
   purple, green, and blue
space to gather the
   children

*Children will learn about colors as they enjoy
singing and moving to a new song.*

*Christian Values:* appreciating God's gifts;
   understanding God's creation
*Bible:* Psalm 136:3 (O give thanks to God, for
   God's gifts are good.)

## GETTING READY

• Learn to sing "Rainbow Song."
• Divide the class into five rows, one row
   for each color. Place the shortest children
   on each end and the tallest children in the
   middle to form an arc.

## HOW TO DO IT

• Sing "Rainbow Song" to the children.
   Help them learn to sing it.
• Give the children in each row a different
   color of paper. Tell them to stand and
   hold up their paper when they sing the
   name of their color.

## VARIATIONS

• Children can paint a paper plate for their
   color.
• Wave streamers for each color as the song
   is sung.
• Have children hold a colored card above
   their head and sway as they sing, first to
   the left, then to the right.

## HOW DID IT GO?

• Did this activity help the children to
   remember the names of the colors?
• Could the children remember the
   sequence of colors used in the song?

### Rainbow Song

1. When the rain's al - most done, And you see a lit - tle sun,
2. When the rain's al - most through, And you see a rain - bow, too,

Look up high and all a - round the sky; A rain - bow may be pass - ing by.
Red and yel - low, pur - ple, green and blue; A rain - bow show's that God loves you.

WORDS: Pat Floyd • MUSIC: Traditional • Words © 1987 by Graded Press

# Ring the Bells

Children will learn about the baby Jesus by singing Christmas music.

**Christian Values:** remembering our Christian heritage; responding to God
**Bible:** Psalm 100:1-2 (Make a joyful noise to God; come into his presence with singing.)

## MATERIALS NEEDED

elastic ½ inch wide, cut into 5-inch lengths
Christmas bells
song "Ring, Ring, Christmas Bells"

## GETTING READY
- Stitch two or three bells to each piece of elastic. Sew ends together. Make two bracelets for each child.

## HOW TO DO IT
- Give each child two bracelets. Sing the song for the children.
- Tell the Christmas story and talk about why the people were so happy.
- Guide the children in learning the song so they may sing as they shake their bells.

## VARIATIONS
- Let the children march to see the baby Jesus as they sing and shake their bells.
- Sing the song and play the bells while the children dance around the room with joy.

## HOW DID IT GO?
- How are your children responding to all the stimulation of Christmas? In what ways do you need to adjust your activities or schedule? Did the children enjoy responding to the music?

### Ring, Ring, Christmas Bells

1. Ring, ring, Christ-mas bells, on this morn, tell the world, tell the world that Je - sus is born!
2. Ring, ring, Christ-mas bells, loud and clear, tell the world, tell the world that Je - sus is here!

WORDS and MUSIC: Ruth Folta Snogren•ARRANGEMENT: Timothy Edmonds
© 1970 by Graded Press • Arrangement © 1992 by Cokesbury

# The Recycle Band

## MATERIALS NEEDED

variety of plastic and metal containers (chip cans, plastic containers, coffee cans)

fillers such as plastic milk lids, pull-tab juice lids

*Children will use their creativity to make instruments from recycled materials and then enjoy using them to praise God.*

**Christian Values:** caring for God's creation; making music to express thanksgiving

**Bible:** Psalm 150:3-6 (Praise God with instruments and dance.)

## GETTING READY

- Assemble shakers. Use a variety of sound combinations by putting metal with metal, plastic with plastic, and so on. Seal tightly or tape closed. Filler should be child-safe in case instrument accidently opens.

## HOW TO DO IT

- Hold up some of the plastic containers and let the children tell what they are and how they were used. Say: "Today we will use recycled cans that have been made into instruments."
- Give each child an instrument. Play by holding it with both hands and shaking it in rhythm with the music.
- Use the music as you thank God for all good gifts. Name one thing, then play a few bars; name another blessing, and repeat the pattern.

## VARIATIONS

- Play instruments with the children's favorite songs of praise. Recycle old Sunday school packet records for good music to use.
- *For older children:* Help the children make up a song about taking care of God's world when everyone helps recycle. Play the instruments as you sing the song.
- Let older children make and decorate their own instruments.

## HOW DID IT GO?

- Were children able to coordinate stopping their playing of the instruments with the stopping of the recorded music?

# Express Praise

Children will praise God with body movement or by playing instruments.

**Christian Values:** expressing praise and thanksgiving to God

**Bible:** Psalm 47:1 (Express your joy to God.)

## MATERIALS NEEDED

song "Clap, Clap"
bells
drum
sticks
tambourine

## GETTING READY
- Learn the song "Clap, Clap."
- Place instruments on the table.

## HOW TO DO IT
- Introduce the song. Children listen the first time through and then follow the actions the second time.
- Possible actions:
  Wave your arms.
  Stamp your feet.
  Pat your knees.
  Touch your toes.

## VARIATIONS
- *For younger children:* Give each child a pair of sticks and sing "Tap, tap, tap your sticks."
- *For older children:* Use all of the rhythm instruments together: ring your bells, tap your sticks, beat your drums, shake your tambourine.
- Ask older children to add their own verses such as "Snap your fingers."

## HOW DID IT GO?
- Did the children follow the actions?
- Could the children think of other motions to do?

**Clap, Clap**

Clap, clap, clap your hands. Clap, clap, clap your thanks to God.

WORDS: Psalm 47:1 (adapted) • MUSIC: Cecilia Williams • © 1977 by Graded Press

## MATERIALS NEEDED

chart tablet
markers
song "Let Us Love One
   Another"

# Show Love

*Children will identify ways they show love to others and sing a song of praise.*

*Christian Values:* showing love to others
*Bible:* Ephesians 4:25b, 32 (In the Christian community, we belong to one another and should love one another.)

## GETTING READY
• Learn the song "Let Us Love One Another."

## HOW TO DO IT
• Guide children to think of ways they can show love. List ideas on a chart.
• Teach "Let Us Love One Another." Sing it once while the children listen.
• When the children have learned the song, ask three children to say quickly something they can do to show love.

## VARIATIONS
• *For younger children:* Use this experience in moments of worship and follow it by saying a prayer of thanks.
• Pantomime acts of love and have children guess what they are.
• *For older children:* Draw pictures that illustrate ways to show love.

## HOW DID IT GO?
• Was the song more meaningful when the children thought of ways they could show love?

### Let Us Love One Another

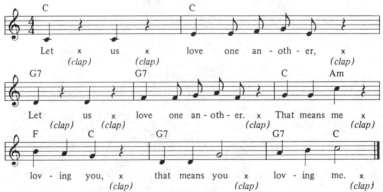

WORDS: Ann F. Price, based on Romans 12:10 • MUSIC: Ann F. Price • © 1981 by Ann F. Price

# Concentration

## MATERIALS NEEDED

ten pairs of cards with
  pictures of birds,
  animals, insects, and so
  on
extra pairs if more than
  two children play

*Children will grow in appreciation of and be able to name some of God's creatures.*

*Christian Values:* understanding God's creation; valuing others
*Bible:* Genesis 1:31 (God saw everything made and it was good.)

## GETTING READY
• Cut out or draw two identical pictures for each set of cards.

## HOW TO DO IT
• Gather a small group of children at a table or on the floor.
• Lay the cards face down. The first child chooses two cards and turns them over so all can see. If they match, the child keeps them as a pair. If not, the cards are turned face down and the next child has a turn.
• Continue the game until all the cards are paired. Winning is not the emphasis. Finding all of the pairs is the goal.

## VARIATIONS
• *For younger children:* Use common animals that a child is familiar with. Let a child choose a card and tell what the picture is.
• *For older children:* Use the cards to learn the names of the creatures. Each child chooses a card from the pile. Those who chose the same cards say the names of the creatures.

## HOW DID IT GO?
• What did you learn about the children as they played (attention span, taking turns, retaining knowledge, and so on)?
• Was the game effective in helping children learn new creatures?

## MATERIALS NEEDED

construction paper
sidewalk or level area
    outside
scissors

# Beauty Spot

*Children will prepare a beauty spot near the classroom.*

**Christian Values:** developing creativity; expressing appreciation for God's beautiful earth

**Bible:** Ecclesiastes 3:11 (God has made everything beautiful.)

## GETTING READY

- Plan a nature walk on level ground where children can find a variety of beauty items.
- Make a construction paper frame for each child. Cut out the inside of a piece of paper leaving a 1-inch border.
- Recruit extra adults to supervise.

## HOW TO DO IT

- Tell children that they will make a "beauty square" picture.
- Distribute frames. Allow children to place their square frame on the ground.
- Help them describe or name the beautiful things within their picture frame (dandelions, grass, flowers, bugs).

## VARIATIONS

- Take a nature walk and collect some nature items such as flowers, leaves, or small rocks to make another kind of "beauty square." Show children how to arrange the nature items on a piece of lightweight cardboard within the frame to make a beautiful scene. Glue items in place or tape a piece of cellophane wrap over the picture.
- Take a picture of each beauty square and post the pictures on the bulletin board.

## HOW DID IT GO?

- Was it hard for children to create something that could not be taken home?
- Encourage them to do it again on their own.

# Ceiling Stars

## MATERIALS NEEDED

flashlight
aluminum pie pan
dark scarf or fabric piece
masking tape
resting mats or sheets
scissors
colored cellophane

*Children will relax and talk about some of God's gifts of nature.*

*Christian Values:* experiencing the orderliness of God's plan; trusting God
*Bible:* Genesis 1:5 (God called the light Day and the darkness Night.)

## GETTING READY
• Use a large nail and hammer to punch holes in the pie pan bottom.
• Tape the scarf around the pan edge so that it hangs down from the pan like a skirt.

## HOW TO DO IT
• Have children lie on mats or sheets on their backs. Dim the lights.
• Have a teacher or child turn the flashlight on and hold it under the pan and fabric cover. Shine it upward through the bottom of the pan so that the "stars" appear on the ceiling.
• Move the pan so that stars move in slow graceful patterns.

## VARIATIONS
• Play music as the children look at the "stars" or sing songs about nighttime.
• Cut circles of colored cellophane and place inside the pie pan so that the ceiling stars appear colored.

• Make one hole larger than the others. Let the children lie down and watch the stars move across the ceiling as you tell the Christmas story.

## HOW DID IT GO?
• Were the children able to relax and wonder over God's creation?
• Were all the children comfortable with darkening the room?

## MATERIALS NEEDED

5 clear plastic jars
about a cup of
  rich soil
  clay soil
  sandy soil
  fine gravel
  rocks
water

# Discover the Good Earth

*Children will examine and observe various forms of the natural world.*

**Christian Values:** appreciating God's creation
**Bible:** Genesis 1:10 (God called the dry land Earth and the waters Sea.)

## GETTING READY

- Fill each jar a third full with a different kind of soil.

## HOW TO DO IT

- Guide the children in a comparison discussion of the different kinds of earth. Ask: "How are they alike?" "How are they different?" "In which jar do you think seeds would grow?"
- Fill jars half full with water. Shake the jars and observe what happens.
- As the children watch the jars, ask: "What is happening now?" "Why is the dirt sinking to the bottom?" "What will happen if we shake the jars again?"

## VARIATIONS

- *For younger children:* Compare two types of soil.
- *For older children:* Expand the experiment by planting bean seeds in each jar and observing the growth over several weeks.
- Express awe and wonder at the differences in God's creation.

## HOW DID IT GO?

- What evidence did you have that the children were thinking as they were observing?
- Could they make conclusions from their observations?

SCIENCE DEVELOPMENT • THINKING SKILLS

# Don't Pollute

## MATERIALS NEEDED

a large picture of a park with a lake, cut from a calendar or poster

candy wrappers, soda cans, bottles, hot dog wrappers, and so on

container to use as a "trash can"

a large plastic swimming pool

*Children will learn about caring for God's world by helping keep the environment clean.*

**Christian Values:** respecting and caring for God's world; being helpful

**Bible:** Genesis 2:15 (God made us responsible for caring for the world.)

## GETTING READY
- Display the picture near the swimming pool.
- Put water in the swimming pool.

## HOW TO DO IT
- Look at the picture and the swimming pool. Talk about how pretty the "lake" is and how clean the water is.
- Give each child some "clean" trash.
- Make up a story of people coming to the park and throwing trash in the lake (include your trash items).
- Whenever you name the kind of trash the child has, he or she throws that piece into the "lake."
- Talk about what happens when people do not care for the lake. Ask what needs to be done to make it the way God created it.

## VARIATIONS
- Walk around the building and pick up trash and debris.
- Decorate the trash cans in your own room.

## HOW DID IT GO?
- Are the children more cooperative about cleaning up?
- Did the children relate their own experiences in the park?

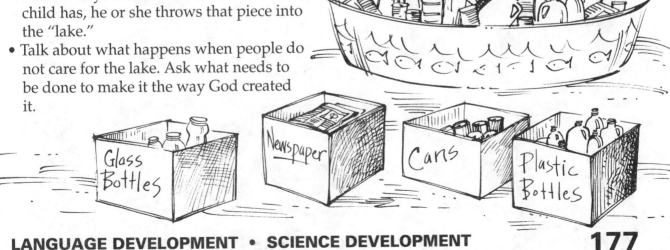

## MATERIALS NEEDED

appropriate music
record player or tape
player

# Gardening Movement

*Children will act out movements used in gardening as one way of caring for God's world.*

**Christian Values:** appreciating the wonder of God's creation; caring for God's creation
**Bible:** Ecclesiastes 3:11 (God made everything beautiful in its time.)

## GETTING READY
• Prepare a large space so children can move freely.

## HOW TO DO IT
• Play appropriate music and use body movement to dramatize gardening: digging, planting, weeding, watering, and harvesting. Try doing the activity outdoors.
• Say a prayer of thanks for God's plan for food.

## VARIATIONS
• Pretend to plant specific foods for health, which will be served that day for snack or lunch. See activity on page 64.
• Encourage children to roleplay wheat blowing in the breeze, carrots growing straight up under the ground, or apples falling from the tree and rolling on the ground.

## HOW DID IT GO?
• Did the children show that they were familiar with a variety of ways plants grow?

# Pine-cone Tray

## MATERIALS NEEDED

pine cones
tempera paint
glue
oval board made of
   plywood or corrugated
   board
empty margarine or cream
   cheese tubs
brushes

*Children will care for the world by recycling pine cones to make something useful.*

*Christian Values:* being good stewards; developing creative skills
*Bible:* Genesis 2:15 (God made us responsible for caring for the world.)

## GETTING READY
• Collect clean, good pine cones.
• Have the boards cut the shape you want.
• Mix the tempera paints.

## HOW TO DO IT
• Give each child a board and enough pine cones to go around the outside of it.
• Let the children choose their paint color and paint the tips of the cones.
• When dry, arrange them around the edge of the board and glue them in place.
• Use the tray for a fruit dish.

## VARIATIONS
• *For younger children:* Tear off the petals of the pine cones.
• Glue them around the sides of the magarine tubs. Use for a candy or nut dish.

## HOW DID IT GO?
• Were most of the children satisfied with their work?
• Are the children beginning to be aware of ways to recycle?

**CREATIVE ART • SMALL-MUSCLE SKILLS**

# Plant Seeds

## MATERIALS NEEDED

waterproof table covering
small peat pots or
  disposable cups
seeds (vegetable, flower,
  fruit)
potting soil
large spoons for digging
spray bottle of water
plastic wrap
rubber bands
children's smocks

*Children will become aware of God's plan for growth by planting and caring for seeds.*

*Christian Values:* understanding and caring for God's creation
*Bible:* Genesis 1:11, 31a (God created plants that bear seeds and saw that it was good.)

## GETTING READY
• Cover a table with a waterproof covering.
• Assemble all the materials.
• Plan to work together in small groups.

## HOW TO DO IT
• Each child will fill a pot with soil.
• Scoop out a hole in the middle, plant the seed, and cover it.
• Use the spray bottle to water the seeds.
• Cover the pot with plastic wrap and secure with a rubber band.
• Place the pot in a shady place until the seeds sprout. Uncover and move the pot to a sunny spot.
• Talk with the children about God's plan for plants to grow from seeds.

## VARIATIONS
• *For younger children:* Plant all the seeds in a baking pan or muffin tin and let the children take turns caring for them.
• *For older children:* Plant the seeds outside and let children take care of them.
• Take photographs to record the growth of the seeds and use pictures to make a chart.

## HOW DID IT GO?
• How do you know the children are beginning to understand God's plan for growth?
• In what ways were you able to relate the activity to the Bible passage?
• Were there opportunities to say spontaneous prayers?

*1.*

*2.*

*3.*

**SCIENCE DEVELOPMENT • SMALL-MUSCLE SKILLS**

# Save Our Earth

## MATERIALS NEEDED

can full of presorted trash
newspaper
labeled boxes for sorted
trash

*Children will understand that the importance of recycling is to save our beautiful world.*

**Christian Values:** preserving God's creation; using resources wisely
**Bible:** Genesis 1 (God created a beautiful world for us, and it is good.)

## GETTING READY

- Prepare a can of trash including different kinds of paper, plastics, bottles, and cans. Cover part of the floor with newspaper.
- Collect information about recycling and landfills.

## HOW TO DO IT

- Explain the terms *recycle* and *landfill*. Say: "Today we will find out how many things we are throwing away that could be used again. If we make less trash, our landfills won't be so full."
- Dump out all the trash on the floor. Sort the trash into labeled boxes: paper, bottles, cardboard, aluminum, and newspaper.
- Find a person to be responsible for taking the trash to a recycling center, or take a field trip with the children (page 219).

## VARIATIONS

- Make a picture graph of how many bottles, paper towels, and other products were in the trash can.
- Make a list of ways that your class can make less waste: use smaller pieces of paper towels to dry hands, use newspaper for painting, or use scraps of construction paper for new projects.
- Tell children that if we don't recycle, soon there may be less space for God's beautiful trees and flowers to grow.

## HOW DID IT GO?

- Do children have a better understanding of recycling?
- Can the children recycle at home?

Bottles

Newspapers

Plastic

Aluminum

**THINKING SKILLS • SCIENCE DEVELOPMENT**

**181**

## MATERIALS NEEDED

3 large sheets of tagboard or bulletin-board paper
crayons or colored chalk
construction paper in fall colors
scissors
glue

# A Classroom Seasonal Tree

*Children will become aware of seasonal changes as they change their classroom tree.*

*Christian Values:* understanding God's plan for seasons; caring for God's creation

*Bible:* Genesis 8:22 (God promises there will always be a time for spring, summer, fall, and winter.)

## GETTING READY

- Cut a basic tree shape and branches from tagboard. Make the tree as large as your space allows, or cut the tree out in three sections and tape it together.
- Color the tree with brown crayons or chalk. Spray chalk with clear shellac.
- Mount the tree on a bulletin board or wall. Be creative with your tree. Draw a squirrel hole in the trunk, put pumpkins under a fall tree, or add a bird's nest made from tissue paper.

## HOW TO DO IT

- Children change the tree each season, adjusted to your geographic area.
- *Fall:* Children trace leaf patterns onto red, yellow, or orange construction paper and cut them out. Glue these to the tree branches.

## VARIATIONS

- *Winter:* Remove the fall leaves and cover branches with cotton batting for snow.
- *Spring:* Remove cotton. Children can roll up small green tissue-paper squares to look like buds and glue these onto tree.
- *Summer:* Remove the buds. Cut green leaves from construction paper.

## HOW DID IT GO?

- Can the children name the four seasons and relate the natural changes of the tree?

**SCIENCE DEVELOPMENT • THINKING SKILLS**

# Space Play

## MATERIALS NEEDED

large paper bags
strong plastic bags for
  ankle weights
sand
bandannas
scissors
markers

*Children will be sensitive to experiences of space travel and the orderliness of God's plans for creation.*

*Christian Values:* respecting creation; being sensitive to the orderliness of God's plan
*Bible:* Acts 17:24 (God made the world and everything in it.)

## GETTING READY

- Have materials available for dramatic play center.

## HOW TO DO IT

- Draw face holes on paper sacks to make the space helmets. Children can cut out the face holes.
- Talk about the laws of gravity and why people cannot walk easily on the moon. What happens to the astronaut? How are persons able to walk?
- Make ankle weights by letting children fill the plastic bags with sand. Wrap a filled bag in a bandanna and tie it loosely around the child's ankle.
- Form a rocket ship out of chairs.
- Plan ample clear space for walking on the moon. Use masking tape on the floor to help children see the boundaries for their play.

## VARIATIONS

- *For younger children:* Take the class on a space ride together using the rocket ship built with chairs.
- Look through paper-towel-tube telescopes to discover the earth. See God's wonders by visiting a park, the hills, the desert, or the seashore.

## HOW DID IT GO?

- What new language did the children use that indicated their familiarity with space?

## MATERIALS NEEDED

a safe place of beauty to walk
extra adults to talk with the children as they walk
paper sack for each child
tape recorder and tape

# Take a Wonder Walk

*Children will experience wonder by using their senses outdoors.*

*Christian Values:* appreciating God's creation; responding to God
*Bible:* Genesis 1:1, 31a (God created the heavens and the earth and saw that it was good.)

## GETTING READY

- Talk with the children about where you will walk.
- Talk about some of God's wonders to see, smell, or hear.
- Encourage children to use their eyes, noses, and ears on this walk.

## HOW TO DO IT

- Take the children outside in small groups. As you walk, encourage children to look at, listen to, and sniff some of God's wonders in the natural world.
- Talk with the children about what you discovered.
- Let the children lead you to wonders that you may have overlooked.

## VARIATIONS

- Take a tape recorder with you to record sounds.
- Give the children sacks in which to collect wonders.
- Make a wonder book when you return to class.

## HOW DID IT GO?

- What evidence did you see that the children experienced wonder?
- What surprises did you find in God's world today?
- How can this activity help children empathize with blind children? How would it feel not to be able to see? or hear?

# Bug Catchers

Children will observe insects and understand why living things must be set free.

*Christian Values:* appreciating God's creation; caring for creation
*Bible:* Genesis 1:25 (God created every living creature and it was good.)

## MATERIALS NEEDED

cylindrical oatmeal boxes with lids
screen netting
craft glue

## GETTING READY
- Cut a 3- by 3-inch square shape from the side of an oatmeal box.
- Securely tape or glue a piece of screen netting over the square.
- Take a walk outside and capture a safe insect.
- Place the insect in the oatmeal observation box. Replace the lid.

## HOW TO DO IT
- Help children discover insects found in your area by looking at pictures or reading stories about them.
- Talk about insects as valuable living creatures (they eat harmful bugs, cross-pollinate flowers, keep the balance of nature).
- Let the children take turns looking at the insect in the observation box.
- After each child has had a turn, let the insect go. Watch as it returns to nature.

## VARIATIONS
- Make insect observation boxes that the children can take home. Ask parents to help the children capture insects that may be brought to school.
- Look for beetles, moths, or dragonflies under small rocks or near flowers.

## HOW DID IT GO?
- Have children learned to value all forms of life, no matter how small and insignificant they may seem?

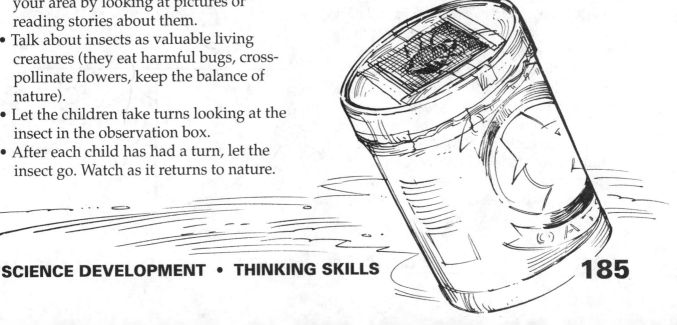

**SCIENCE DEVELOPMENT • THINKING SKILLS**

# The Butterfly Cycle

*Children will become aware of God's plan for the cycle of the butterfly and make a picture graph of it.*

*Christian Values:* finding wonder in God's creation; expressing creativity

*Bible:* Ecclesiastes 3:11 (God has made everything beautiful.)

## MATERIALS NEEDED

white, brown, and green construction paper
small pieces of tissue
cotton balls
⅓ piece of pipe cleaner for each child
felt-tip markers
page 19 for making butterflies

## GETTING READY

- Cut large leaves from green paper.
- Draw a large circle on each child's white paper; divide into four equal parts.
- Cut branch shapes out of brown paper.
- Cut pipe cleaners into thirds for caterpillars. (One per child.)

## HOW TO DO IT

- **Stage 1:** Say: *Butterflies lay eggs on the leaf.* Children place a green leaf in the first space, ball a small piece of tissue paper to make an egg, and glue it to the leaf.
- **Stage 2:** Say: *Caterpillars hatch from the eggs and eat the leaf.* Children place a leaf in the second space, poke one end of a pipe-cleaner piece into the leaf, let it hump, and then glue the other end onto the leaf.
- **Stage 3:** Say: *Caterpillars spin a cocoon.* Children glue a branch in the third space and glue a cotton ball to it. Show how to pull it down to look like a cocoon.
- **Stage 4:** Say: *After many days the butterfly will hatch.* Children can make a butterfly and glue onto the fourth space.

## VARIATIONS

- *For older children*: Emphasize the math concept of one-to-one relationship with egg–caterpillar–cocoon–butterfly.

## HOW DID IT GO?

- Can the children identify the four stages of the butterfly cycle?

# Crazy Caterpillars

*Children will understand and enjoy learning about caterpillars.*

*Christian Values:* learning about God's creatures; praising God for creation

*Bible:* Psalm 8:6-8 (God made many creatures to live in the fields, air, and sea.)

## MATERIALS NEEDED

small paper plates
tempera paints
paintbrushes
paint smocks
pipe cleaners
paper punch
yarn
newspapers

## GETTING READY
• Place paint, brushes, and paper plates on a table covered with newspaper.

## HOW TO DO IT
• Tell children: "Today we will make a caterpillar for our classroom."
• Allow children to choose a color and paint their paper plates.
• Use a plate for the head of the caterpillar. Paint on eyes and a nose and glue on two pipe cleaners for the antennae.
• Punch holes in the plates and tie them together to make a long caterpillar.
• Display the caterpillar in the classroom.

## VARIATIONS
• Circles may be cut out of construction paper instead of using paper plates.
• Show real caterpillars if they are available.
• Check your library for the book *The Very Hungry Caterpillar* by Eric Carle. Tell the story to the children as you show them the delightful pictures.

## HOW DID IT GO?
• Did the children seem enthusiastic as they saw their plates being put together to make a long caterpillar?

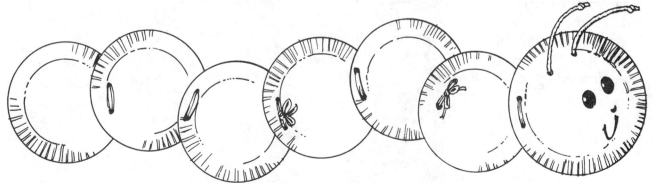

## MATERIALS NEEDED

a container of earthworms
from a bait-and-tackle
store, or dug from a
garden or compost pile
construction paper cut into
worm shapes
markers or crayons

# Earthworm Day

*Children will appreciate one of God's most unnoticed but important creatures.*

*Christian Values:* appreciating God's creation; understanding God's creation
*Bible:* Genesis 1:25 (God made every creeping creature and it was good.)

## GETTING READY

- Read about earthworms and their benefits in an encyclopedia or a reference book.
- Prepare a large box lid or pan with dirt. Spread out the worms in the pan.
- Gather construction paper worms and markers or crayons.

## HOW TO DO IT

- Show the earthworms to the children. Allow the children to touch them.
- Discuss the important role of an earthworm, especially in gardening (makes air tunnels in dirt, fertilizes earth).
- Distribute earthworms cut from construction paper. Have children decorate the worms as desired.

## VARIATIONS

- Any living creatures may be used for study instead of earthworms!

## HOW DID IT GO?

- Were children fearful to see and touch the worms? How can you help them overcome these fears?
- What evidence do you have that the children grew in their understanding of God's creation and how worms are helpful.

**SCIENCE DEVELOPMENT**

# Firefly Lights

## MATERIALS NEEDED

flashlights or penlights
(one for each child, or
one for each small group
of children)

*Children will enjoy pretending to be fireflies and learning a verse about fireflies.*

*Christian Values:* enjoying fellowship;
  appreciating God's gift of nature
*Bible:* Genesis 1:25 (God created all living
  things and called it good.)

## GETTING READY
- Learn the words to the fingerplay.
- Practice turning on the flashlights each time you say the word *light.*

## HOW TO DO IT
- Distribute flashlights and teach the fingerplay.
- Children will turn on the flashlight each time they say the word *light.*

## VARIATIONS
- *For younger children:* The teacher may need to use the flashlight as children say the rhyme.
- Use a classroom light or lamp instead of flashlights.

## HOW DID IT GO?
- Did children feel good about participating in the fingerplay?
- If children had difficulty remembering, how can you increase their attention span?

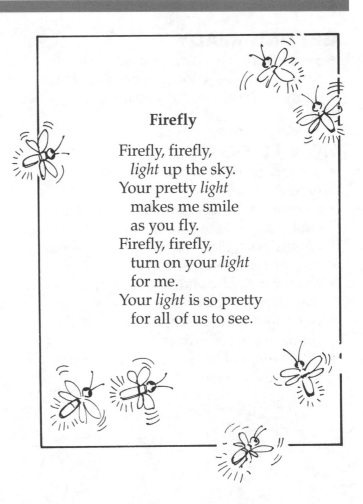

**Firefly**

Firefly, firefly,
  *light* up the sky.
Your pretty *light*
  makes me smile
  as you fly.
Firefly, firefly,
  turn on your *light*
  for me.
Your *light* is so pretty
  for all of us to see.

**LANGUAGE DEVELOPMENT • SCIENCE DEVELOPMENT**

## MATERIALS NEEDED

16 to 20 half-pint milk or juice cartons with tops cut off
white glue
adhesive paper
collection of small nature items (rock, feather, leaf, shell, and so on)
magnifying glass

# A Discovery Museum

*Children will examine, feel wonder at, and appreciate items from our natural world.*

*Christian Values:* experiencing wonder and appreciation for God's creation; respecting others

*Bible:* Psalm 104:24 (God has made many wonderful things.)

## GETTING READY

• Staple or glue the cartons together to form a set of cubicles. Glue a few at a time and let them dry. Cover the outside with adhesive paper.

## HOW TO DO IT

• Encourage children and parents to bring nature treasures to the museum.
• As children bring nature items, label the cubbie space with a name and the name of the object. Place each child's treasures on a piece of construction paper.
• Show the children how to use a magnifying glass and put it away.
• Talk about care and appreciation for the contributions of each child.
• Offer words of praise and thanksgiving for God's creation.

## VARIATIONS

• *For younger children:* With 2- and 3-year-olds labeling is not necessary. Verbally identify the objects.
• *For older children*: Labeling items helps them learn names and associate words with objects. It also helps to teach respect for others' treasures.

## HOW DID IT GO?

• Are the children enjoying sharing and displaying their nature objects?
• In what ways are they showing care and respect?

# Living Things Change

*Children will discover that God plans for living things to grow and change.*

*Christian Values:* understanding that God's creation grows in an orderly way; praising God
*Bible:* Matthew 6:28 (Lilies of the field grow.)

## MATERIALS NEEDED

matching picture cards of things that change, such as egg–chicken, seed–flower
sequencing pictures of things that grow, at least four sets: seed–seedling, tree with apple blossoms–tree with apples

## GETTING READY
- Draw matching pictures of things that change (check class packets).
- Find a story about growing, such as *The Carrot Seed*, by Ruth Krauss.

## HOW TO DO IT
- Give each child a picture card of the initial stage of a living thing.
- Lay the pictures of the grown object face up on the floor or a table.
- Ask each child to show his or her picture to the group, name it, and choose the picture that shows what it grew into.
- Encourage the children to talk about their pictures. "The egg became a chicken."

## VARIATIONS
- *For older children:* Have the children arrange four growth pictures in sequence. Encourage them to tell about the process in story form.
- Keep the cards in a box and leave them out for the children to play with later.

## HOW DID IT GO?
- Did the children show some understanding of the growth process?
- Do they enjoy using the pictures on their own?

## MATERIALS NEEDED

cutouts of animals and
   fruit
black construction paper
scissors
glue

# Matching Game

*Children will develop the ability to match a picture with its silhouette.*

**Christian Values:** developing God's gift of thinking; thanking God for our minds
**Bible:** Proverbs 2:6 (God gives wisdom.)

## GETTING READY

- Select pictures of animals and fruit from magazines or curriculum. Cut around each animal or fruit.
- Make a silhouette of each animal or fruit shape from black construction paper.
- Glue each picture and silhouette on 5½- by 8-inch cards.

## HOW TO DO IT

- Put the picture shapes and the silhouettes in two separate containers. Ask the children to pick one picture shape, name it, and then find its silhouette from the other box.

## VARIATIONS

- *For older children:* Use more complicated pictures to make it more difficult to match the silhouette.
- Use two silhouettes, but of two different colors, for matching.

## HOW DID IT GO?

- How did the younger children respond to the activity? Were they frustrated when they could not do the activity?
- Do the children choose this activity to do during their free play?

**THINKING SKILLS • SMALL-MUSCLE SKILLS**

# Here Comes the Wind

*Children will learn about weather conditions as a part of God's plan of creation.*

**Christian Values:** appreciating God's creation; overcoming fears

**Bible:** Genesis 8:1 (God made the wind to blow over the earth.)

---

## MATERIALS NEEDED

two 3-foot crepe-paper streamers per child
12-inch dowel for each child
glue

---

## GETTING READY
- Limit the number of children working at one time.

## HOW TO DO IT
- Talk about God's creation of the wind. Sometimes when it blows very hard, people stay indoors for fear of being hurt. Encourage children to talk about their experiences.
- To watch the wind blow, make a streamer by gluing two crepe-paper strips together at one end.
- Wrap the glued end around a dowel and glue in place.
- Outdoors, hold the dowel up, allowing the streamers to blow in the wind.

## VARIATIONS
- Pretend to be leaves swaying as the "Wind" says "I'm blowing gently." When the Wind says "I'm blowing hard," the leaves fall to the ground.

- Tie the streamers on the lower limbs of trees, bushes, or poles and watch them dance in the wind.

## HOW DID IT GO?
- What evidence is there that the children are feeling more secure about the wind?
- Did the children express how they feel about windy weather?

# Nature Patterns

*Children will recognize and build on visual patterns.*

**Christian Values:** enhancing self-esteem; recognizing God's creation
**Bible:** Psalm 103:22 (In every place, praise God for all of creation.)

## MATERIALS NEEDED

flannelboard
pieces of felt
scissors

## GETTING READY
• Cut felt into shapes found in nature, such as the sun, moon, stars or flowers, trees, leaves. Make at least eight of each shape.

## HOW TO DO IT
• Begin at top left of a flannelboard and put up a simple pattern, such as star-moon-star-moon.
• Ask the children what picture should come next. Point to and name each picture, going from left to right.
• Name the pattern in a chanting voice. This may help children follow the pattern.

## VARIATIONS
• *For younger children:* Place a pattern on the flannelboard. Let the children match the pattern by placing a row of felt pieces below the pattern row.

• *For older children:* Make patterns more challenging for those who understand the concept. Encourage children to make up their own patterns and then copy them on the next row.

## HOW DID IT GO?
• Did reading the pattern as a chant help children understand the repetition of pictures in the pattern?

**THINKING SKILLS • MATH READINESS**

# Ribbon Mobile

## MATERIALS NEEDED

colorful, lightweight fabric
large plastic hoop
white school glue
strong cord
scissors

*Children will work together in making a project to explore the effects of the wind.*

**Christian Values:** exploring God's plan for the wind; working cooperatively
**Bible:** Job 37:14 (Consider the wonderful things God does.)

## GETTING READY
• Cut or tear fabric into strips 3 inches wide and 2 to 3 feet long.

## HOW TO DO IT
• Let children select fabric strips, wrap several inches of each strip over the plastic hoop, and glue to the hoop and fabric.
• When the glue is thoroughly dry, attach strong cords to the hoop at four places and tie the ends together.
• Let the children help hang the hoop in a breezy spot. Measure the strength of the wind by how much and how high the ribbons are blown. Talk about how the wind helps people. What makes the wind blow?

## VARIATIONS
• Let children make individual projects to take home. Use small circles such as a large whipped-topping container lid with the center cut out to leave a circle.
• Go outside and observe other ways the wind is blowing (leaves blowing, laundry on line blowing, hair blowing, papers blowing on street, and so on).

## HOW DID IT GO?
• Can the children identify other ways we know the wind is blowing?
• See the activity on page 193.

## MATERIALS NEEDED

small cups
a variety of small items to
fit the containers such as
cotton ball, stone,
button, soil, sponge,
tissue, crayon, paper,
foil, paper clip, twig,
plastic, screw, paper
towel
eye dropper
cup of water

# Soak It Up!

*Children will discover what materials will absorb or not absorb water.*

*Christian Values:* exploring wonders of God's creation; learning about the dependability of God's laws of creation
*Bible:* Psalm 65:9-10 (The rain water fills the streams and soaks into the soil.)

## GETTING READY
• Place each item in a small cup.
• Have water and eye dropper ready.

## HOW TO DO IT
• Discuss the words *soak* and *absorb*.
• Show the children how to use the eye dropper.
• Children will put drops of water on each item and observe what happens.
• What things soak up the water and which ones do not? Will they soak up water each time?

## VARIATIONS
• *For younger children:* Children will delight in watching the water disappear.
• *For older children:* Graph the results of what absorbs and what does not. Is it consistent?

## HOW DID IT GO?
• Were the children able to use the eye dropper independently?
• What responses indicated the ability to observe and draw a conclusion?

**SCIENCE DEVELOPMENT • THINKING SKILLS**

# Weather Suitcase

*Children will relate types of weather and seasonal changes to appropriate clothing and activities.*

**Christian Values:** understanding God's creation; working with God

**Bible:** Psalm 147:8, 16-18 (God's continuing creation of the natural world includes clouds, rain, snow, ice, and wind.)

## MATERIALS NEEDED

pictures illustrating different weather and seasons
small suitcase
*Fall:* sweater, rain boots, rain coat, football
*Winter:* winter hat, scarf, mittens, snow boots, sled
*Spring:* long jeans, jacket, kite, skates
*Summer:* sandals, shorts, T-shirt, sunglasses, swimsuit

## GETTING READY
- Gather items appropriate for your area and place in a suitcase or totebag.
- Display weather and season pictures.

## HOW TO DO IT
- Use this activity with a small group of children as you study the weather or seasons.
- Let children unpack the suitcase and display the items in the center of a circle.
- Line up four seasonal pictures and have children place items under the pictures.
- Guide the children in classifying the items in the following ways:
  —Items used in different kinds of weather.
  —Items played with in different seasons.
  —Items worn in different climates.

## VARIATIONS
- *For younger children:* Use fewer items.
- Encourage children to think of other weather-related items.
- *For older children:* Make a graph of the items for each season.

## HOW DID IT GO?
- What evidence did you have that the children were thinking through the classifications?

## MATERIALS NEEDED

new children's
  toothbrushes
transportation
extra adults

# Visit With a Dentist

*Children will learn how to care for their teeth and gums by visiting the dentist.*

*Christian Values:* caring for our bodies; appreciating people who help us
*Bible:* Luke 4:38-40 (Jesus healed many people.)

## GETTING READY

- Arrange with your dentist or hygienist to visit the dental office.
- Make a short visit to the dentist's office to check for safety and for suggestions from the dentist.
- Discuss ahead of time with the dentist the questions children have.

## HOW TO DO IT

- Take this trip after children have had some instruction in dental health. Teach the basics about taking care of teeth and gums.
- On the day of the visit, help the dentist guide the tour to best meet the needs and age levels of your group.
- Encourage children to ask questions and talk about their fears of going to the dentist.

## VARIATIONS

- *For younger children:* Arrange for a dentist to come to the classroom.
- Have new toothbrushes for the children to practice brushing teeth.
- Children will enjoy pretending to care for the teeth of their dolls.
- *For older children:* Draw or paint posters showing things to do to promote good dental health.

## HOW DID IT GO?

- Were children able to apply their learnings from the dentist to the care of their own teeth?
- Were they able to thank the dentist for the help in caring for their teeth?

# A Doctor or Nurse Visits

*Children will discover that doctors and nurses are people who help us get well and stay healthy.*

**Christian Values:** caring for one another; using gifts to help others; overcoming fear

**Bible:** Romans 12:4-7 (We have different gifts that can be used to help people.)

## MATERIALS NEEDED

stethoscope
tongue depressors
digital thermometer
medical kit
clean, empty pill bottles

## GETTING READY

- Invite a doctor, nurse, or other health care professional to visit.
- Talk with the visitor about the goals for the visit and about the children's age level.
- Ask the visitor to bring a stethoscope, thermometer, and tongue depressor.
- Prepare a clinic or doctor's office in your room.

## HOW TO DO IT

- When the visitor arrives, have the children gather in a comfortable place for conversation.
- Help the visitor by asking questions.
- Encourage children, if they are willing, to let the doctor listen to their hearts or look in their ears.

## VARIATIONS

- Invite the doctor or nurse to stay longer and sit in a center with interested children.
- Let children play doctor and nurse in the clinic using the baby dolls.
- Let the children listen to one another's hearts with the stethoscope.

## HOW DID IT GO?

- Did any children show fear when they were with the doctor or nurse? What can you do to help children overcome these fears?
- Were the children able to relate their own experiences with doctors and nurses?
- What evidence do you see that the children think of doctors and nurses as helpers?

## MATERIALS NEEDED

any special equipment your visitor uses
crutches, blindfold, hearing aid, wheelchair, and other special needs equipment

# Persons With Handicaps

*Children will discover that people with handicapping conditions have special gifts.*

*Christian Values:* realizing God's care for all people; valuing others
*Bible:* 1 Corinthians 13:4 (Love is patient; love is kind.)

## GETTING READY

- Invite someone with a handicapping condition to your class. Choose someone who is comfortable with his or her condition and with children.
- Prepare the children and the room for the visitor.

## HOW TO DO IT

- Show pictures or talk about people who have handicapping conditions. Discuss ways we can be kind to them.
- Dramatize what it is like to be blind or deaf or be unable to walk.
- When the visitor arrives, ask the person to tell about her or his life. If the person cannot talk, ask if she can sign.

## VARIATIONS

- Encourage your visitor to stay longer and relate to the children as they play.

- Show the children a book in Braille, or check your library for "talking books" for the blind.

## HOW DID IT GO?

- What changes in attitude did you notice in the children?
- How did they react to the visitor?

# Visit a Potter

*Children will observe the creation of a vessel on the potter's wheel.*

*Christian Values:* using God's gift of creativity
  for others
*Bible:* Jeremiah 18:1-4 (Pottery was the means by
  which biblical persons made dishes.)

## MATERIALS NEEDED

modeling clay
wax paper
pan of water
old towels

## GETTING READY
• Talk with the children about making
  pottery. Show samples of some pottery.
• Invite a local potter to demonstrate
  making pottery using a potter's wheel.

## HOW TO DO IT
• The potter sets up the potter's wheel.
  Show children how to mix the clay. Show
  some pieces of wet or dry unfinished
  pottery dishes or jugs.
• Give each child a piece of wax paper and
  a ball of clay. Ask the potter to guide
  them in making snakes, balls, bowls,
  animals, and so on.
• Help children understand this was one
  way people made dishes long ago in
  Bible lands.

## VARIATIONS
• *For younger children:* Let children make
  play dough to use for modeling.
• *For older children:* Visit a potter's shop or
  studio. Have the potter show them the
  different methods of using clay.

## HOW DID IT GO?
• What evidence do you have that the
  children enjoyed watching the potter's
  wheel and working with the clay?
• What plans do you have for letting
  children use clay in the
  classroom?

## MATERIALS NEEDED

any special materials your visitor needs

# An Unusual Job

*Children through hearing a story will realize that people do many kinds of jobs to help others.*

*Christian Values:* appreciating each person's gifts from God that allow us to help others
*Bible:* Romans 12:6-7 (Let us use the different gifts God gave us.)

## GETTING READY

- Invite a woman community helper with an unusual job (such as a telephone line repair person) to visit the class and tell a story about her job.
- Request that the worker bring some tools used in that vocation. Ask her to tell about her work by telling a story.

## HOW TO DO IT

- Seat the children comfortably where the visitor is close and visible to all.
- Ask the visitor to tell a story about her job and to show the tools she uses. If there's a telephone pole nearby, she may be willing to show the children how she climbs it.

*Warning: Children must not climb the poles or touch the wires.*

## VARIATIONS

- Invite women who work in road construction, a zoo, and other nontraditional occupations to tell their stories.
- Borrow books from the library that tell of women working in jobs usually associated with men.

## HOW DID IT GO?

- How did the children react to the visitor?
- Did the children ask their own questions?

# Invite a Police Officer

*Children will learn to overcome fears of police officers, who are their friends and who help people.*

*Christian Values:* responding to God; caring for others

*Bible:* Romans 12:4-7 (We have different gifts to use for others.)

### MATERIALS NEEDED

special snack for the police officer
books or pictures about police officers
invited police officer, with tools such as whistle, flashlight, walkie-talkie

## GETTING READY
- Tell police officer the date, time, place, and purpose for the visit.
- Let children prepare a special snack.
- Check with parents for any fears children may have of police officers.

## HOW TO DO IT
- Let the children look at the pictures or books and talk about the role of a police officer.
- Have the officer talk about strangers, persons who abuse children, what to do if children get lost, and so on.
- Help children think of questions they would like to ask the visitor related to safety.
- Say a prayer of thanks for police officers and serve the special snack. Thank the officer for coming.

## VARIATIONS
- *For younger children:* Read stories or sing songs about police workers.
- Young children may relate best to a female police officer.
- *For older children:* Take a trip to a police station to talk with several different officers and to see the squad cars.

## HOW DID IT GO?
- Did you observe fears among any of the children? Did the visitor help children overcome any of these fears?
- What evidence was there that children grew in understanding of the ways police officers are workers with God?

## MATERIALS NEEDED

colored posterboards
strips of assorted
    construction paper
scissors or paper cutter
glue

# Visit a Weaver

*Children will grow in appreciation of the art of weaving and discover how this work helps people.*

*Christian Values:* recognizing God's plan for creativity; helping others with our gifts
*Bible:* Proverbs 31:13 (Biblical people wove some of their fabrics by hand.)

## GETTING READY

- Ask a weaver to demonstrate weaving cloth. Have some samples to show. The weaver may also show some plants and berries that are used to dye yarn.
- Cut the posterboard into 12-inch squares for a weaving project. Cut 10-inch slits vertically to form a weaving mat.
- Cut assorted colors of construction paper into 1-inch strips.

## HOW TO DO IT

- The weaver demonstrates the steps for preparing the yarn.
- Show children the loom and involve the children as much as possible.
- Let children weave using the weaving mat and ten strips of paper.
- Demonstrate the over-under motion of the weaving pattern. Glue at each end.

## VARIATIONS

- *For younger children:* With four-year-olds make the weaving mats smaller with fewer and wider strips.

## HOW DID IT GO?

- Were the children attentive and involved in the demonstration? How could they participate more?
- Were the children able to do the weaving project?

**CREATIVE ART • SMALL-MUSCLE SKILLS**

# Vegetable or Fruit Market

*Children will learn to appreciate God's care by selecting vegetables at the market and eating them.*

*Christian Values:* appreciating God's care for us
*Bible:* Genesis 1:29 (God has given us plants for food.)

## MATERIALS NEEDED

large bowls of water
vegetable brushes
knife (teacher)
serrated plastic knives
vegetables
paper plates
money for buying

## GETTING READY

- Study the vegetable and fruit food groups with the children.
- Guide the children in deciding what fruits and vegetables they want to taste. Consider those available in your area.
- Arrange transportation and extra adult help.
- Talk with the children about safety and appropriate behavior at the market.

## HOW TO DO IT

- *For older children:* Form shopping groups of one adult and two or three children. Let each group make one purchase. Suggested purchases: beans to string or break, peas to shell, corn to shuck and clean, or ingredients to make a seasonal salad.
- Return to the classroom and prepare the foods you purchased for a tasting party.

## VARIATIONS

- *For younger children:* Collect and bring to the classroom some seasonal fruits and vegetables. Help children identify various vegetables and fruits. Wash, peel, and slice bites for the children to taste.
- Help the children classify fruits and vegetables using picture cards.
- Take a short walk to a curb market to purchase a pumpkin in the fall.
- Use this field trip in a unit on the food groups.

## HOW DID IT GO?

- How well did the children do identifying the fruits and vegetables?
- Did the children behave appropriately?

## MATERIALS NEEDED

transportation
extra adult helpers
money to buy food

# Fast Food Field Trip

*Children will discover how we are helped by people who prepare foods for us to buy.*

*Christian Values:* learning about important jobs adults do; showing appreciation for food workers

*Bible:* Romans 12:4-7 (We are to use our gifts to help people in the community.)

## GETTING READY

- Arrange a field trip to a local fast food restaurant. Most managers have a plan to safely show children how the restaurant works.
- Children may not be able to get close to the cooking area, but they will see where the deliveries are made and how food is prepared and stored.

## HOW TO DO IT

- Divide children into small groups and assign each group to an adult.
- Review rules for politeness and for safety.
- If the tour seems over the heads of children, help the worker to make it understandable.
- Write a class letter to thank the people for helping you learn about their work.

## VARIATIONS

- If there is no fast food restaurant in your town, visit a regular restaurant or bakery.
- Set up the classroom for a "let's pretend" fast food restaurant. Make chef's hats, pretend burgers, pretend drinks, or ice cream sundaes.

## HOW DID IT GO?

- Did children enjoy seeing the unfamiliar side of such a familiar part of their lives? What jobs did they see people doing? What were the different responsibilities? What happens if one person does not do his or her job well?

# Visit a Fire Station

*Children will discover that firefighters are community helpers by visiting their workplace and hearing about their work.*

**Christian Values:** caring for one another; using gifts to help others

**Bible:** Romans 12:4-7 (We have different gifts that can be used to help others.)

## MATERIALS NEEDED

transportation to the fire station
extra adults to accompany the class

## GETTING READY
- Make arrangements to visit a fire station.
- Talk with the firefighters about the age and understanding of the children and the purpose of the visit.
- Plan for transportation and extra adult help.

## HOW TO DO IT
- Talk with the children about where they are going and why, and about the things they may see.
- Have a firefighter show the children the trucks, the clothes, and the tools they use.
- Encourage children to ask questions.
- Thank the firefighters and return to your classroom.
- Give the children opportunities to talk about or draw about their experiences.

## VARIATIONS
- *For older children:* Ask the firefighters to bring the truck to your school.
- Arrange for the fire marshal to come to your school for a fire drill.

## HOW DID IT GO?
- Did the children recognize firefighters as helpers in your community?
- Are there ways you need to improve your field trips with the children?

## MATERIALS NEEDED

  seeds
  potting soil
  paper cups
  newspapers
  spoons

# Greenhouse or Nursery

*Children will discover and thank God for the many different kinds of plants and will want to care for them.*

*Christian Values:* caring for and appreciating creation; understanding God's plan for new growth

*Bible:* Matthew 6:28 (Consider the lilies of the field.)

## GETTING READY

- Arrange to visit a greenhouse or nursery. Discuss your goals.
- Arrange for transportation, permissions, insurance, and extra adult help.
- With the children set goals, safety rules, and proper manners for the trip.

## HOW TO DO IT

- Arrive on time.
- Focus on different kinds of flowers and their seeds. Wonder at God's plan.
- Compare colors, sizes, and shapes.
- Show the seeds from a variety of plants. Explain that the seed always grows the same kind of plant.
- Demonstrate care for growing plants.
- Help each child plant a fast-growing flower seed in the paper cup to take home.
- Say a prayer to thank God for plants and God's plan for new growth.

## VARIATIONS

- *For younger children:* Collect a variety of plants to create your own nursery.
- Ask the nurseryman to visit the class.
- *For older children:* Walk to visit a home vegetable or flower garden.
- Help children make seed collages.
- Visit the nursery during holidays or seasons to see a variety of plants such as poinsettias and lilies.
- Make a spring picture using a blue wash. See page 38.

## HOW DID IT GO?

- How did the children indicate their appreciation of plant life?
- Were the nursery workers able to communicate well with children?
- How can you help the children be dependable in caring for the seeds?

SCIENCE DEVELOPMENT

# Visit a Grocery Store

*Children will visit a grocery store and see how people work with God.*

**Christian Values:** understanding ways people work with God; appreciating these workers
**Bible:** 1 Corinthians 3:9 (We are workers with God.)

## MATERIALS NEEDED

transportation
adults to supervise
  children
money for purchases

## GETTING READY
- Plan a tour with the manager of your local grocery store or supermarket.
- Talk about what children will see, what workers do, and what children can buy.

## HOW TO DO IT
- Encourage children to share their experiences of going to the grocery.
- Suggest questions that will help the tour guide talk with the children.
- Purchase something to take back to the classroom for a snack. Make note of items children are not familiar with.
- Visit the butcher, the manager, the produce clerk, the sackboy, and other workers. Talk about the work they do.
- Other persons children might see are a truck driver or delivery person, a milkman, a meat inspector, and so on.

## VARIATIONS
- *For younger children:* Take the class in small groups to the grocery store. Let them observe ways persons work.
- *For older children:* Interview some of the workers. When you return to the classroom, write a group story or litany.

## HOW DID IT GO?
- What did the children enjoy most? Can they name some of the workers and the jobs they do?
- How will the children say thank you to the workers at the store? What evidence do you have that they grew in appreciation of people who help others?

## MATERIALS NEEDED

shorts and T-shirts
walking shoes

# Gymnasium

*Children will learn to care for their bodies by experiencing body movement.*

**Christian Values:** caring for our bodies
**Bible:** Genesis 1:26 (People are to care for all life in God's world.)

## GETTING READY
- Contact a local gym that gives instruction in gymnastics.
- Discuss your objectives with the instructor and schedule a time when someone can demonstrate the gymnastic equipment and floor routine.
- Arrange for transportation and extra adult help.
- Communicate with parents the need for shorts, T-shirts, and walking shoes.

## HOW TO DO IT
- Let the children enjoy watching people do the gymnastics demonstration and movement exercises.
- Have the instructor lead the children in body movement and tumbling exercises appropriate for the age group.
- Discuss with the children how exercises help keep our bodies healthy.

## VARIATIONS
- *For younger children:* Invite a physical education specialist to come to the class to lead creative movement or tumbling exercises.
- *For older children:* Use this field trip as an activity for a unit on "Our Bodies" or "Health and Fitness."
- Let children enjoy doing movements with music.

## HOW DID IT GO?
- Did all the children participate in the movement activities?
- What informal activities can you use to give the children exercise outdoors?
- Did the children learn movements that you can use in the classroom or use safely at home?

**LARGE-MUSCLE SKILLS • HEALTH**

# Home Building Site

## MATERIALS NEEDED

*Children will observe carpenters building a home and some of the materials needed.*

*Christian Values:* appreciating talents God gives us; using talents to help others
*Bible:* Romans 12:4-7 (God has given us different gifts that can be used to help people.)

## GETTING READY
- Find a site. Call the contractor and make arrangements for a visit when a plumber, electrician, or bricklayer will be there.
- Secure permission and insurance forms, drivers, and extra adult help.
- Remind children of safety precautions and your goals for the visit.

## HOW TO DO IT
- Be prepared to ask leading questions. Point out the jobs that workers do.
- Show children the basic stages in building a house.
- Observe how the wires, pipes, and insulation are inside the walls.
- Show children different materials used, such as wood, insulation, wire, roofing, and nails.

## VARIATIONS
- *For younger children:* Place samples of building materials in the discovery center. Invite a carpenter to tell the children how these materials are used.
- Borrow a movie from your public library to show.
- *For older children:* Write a group experience story about the field trip and illustrate.
- Write a litany showing the children's appreciation for workers who build homes.

## HOW DID IT GO?
- Identify new insights and learnings the children have gained.
- Were adequate safety precautions taken?

## MATERIALS NEEDED

4-by-6 index cards
familiar grocery items
glue
baskets or bags
scissors
old magazines

# Let's Go Shopping

*Children will become familiar with God's gifts through playing a game.*

*Christian Values:* developing independence; appreciating God's gifts
*Bible:* Job 37:14 (Consider the wonderful things God does.)

## GETTING READY

- Place a low table and food items near the play area to serve as a store.
- Cut out pictures of each food object you have in the "store." Glue one picture per card. Make as many cards as you like.

## HOW TO DO IT

- At circle time, let each child select three picture cards and turn them over on the table to hide the pictures.
- Let the child show the pictures and name the items. Give the child a basket or bag. Tell the child to go "shopping" and bring those items back to you. Have the child give the cards to you to hold.
- If children forget an item, they may come back and look again at the cards.

## VARIATIONS

- Use shoes or clothing items instead of grocery items.
- *For younger children:* If the game is too hard, give each child only two cards or let the child take the card to the grocery store.
- If children are shy, let them work in pairs to pick up the items.
- *For older children:* Let each child cut out pictures from old magazines of foods they see. Glue one food picture on each card.
- If the game is too easy, give more cards.

## HOW DID IT GO?

- Which children had difficulty in remembering? How can you give them extra help in memory skills?
- Which items were not familiar?

**THINKING SKILLS • LANGUAGE DEVELOPMENT**

# Visit a Newspaper

*Children will learn about the world by observing the activities at a newspaper.*

*Christian Values:* learning about God's busy world; appreciating people who help us

*Bible:* Galatians 5:13 (Serve one another in love.)

## MATERIALS NEEDED

transportation to a local newspaper office
adults to supervise the trip
money to buy a newspaper

## GETTING READY

- Schedule a tour with the manager of your local newspaper.
- Arrange for chaperons and transportation.

## HOW TO DO IT

- On the day of the trip, assign small groups of children to each adult.
- Show the newspaper to children during daily lessons, pointing especially to pictures, math symbols, or words they can recognize. Explain how a newspaper helps us to be informed.
- Ask questions of the guide that will help the children understand how the paper is printed.
- Visit the editors of the comics, advertising, news, and religion. Talk about their jobs and how they get news.
- Purchase a finished copy for the children to use in the classroom.

## VARIATIONS

- Visit a local printing shop.
- Since many newspapers are now set up with computers, bring a computer (or typewriter) into the classroom.
- Make a class newspaper with news about the class for the parents to read.
- Write a group story about how a newspaper is printed. Let children illustrate it or take instant photos.

## HOW DID IT GO?

- Were the children interested in each newspaper worker's job?
- Discuss ways this trip helped children to better understand our busy world.

## MATERIALS NEEDED

transportation
adults to chaperon
baskets or bags to collect
fruit

# Visit an Orchard

*Children will visit an orchard to become aware of God's plan for trees and fruit.*

*Christian Values:* appreciating God's creation, learning through the senses
*Bible:* Psalm 98:1 (God has done wonderful things.)

## GETTING READY

- Obtain permission from a local grower to visit an apple, peach, orange, or other fruit orchard.
- Arrange transportation with adequate adult supervision for the children.

## HOW TO DO IT

- Discuss God's plan for fruit.
- Tell children what they will see. Discuss safety rules.
- Show children how the fruit grows. Note size, shape, colors, and the taste of the fruit at various stages of growth.
- If the fruit is in season, let the children gather some fruit and have a taste.
- If fruit is not in season, show pictures or samples of what the fruit looks like when it is mature.
- Purchase some of the fruit at the grocery store and serve as a snack.

## VARIATIONS

- Visit a pumpkin or strawberry patch or some other type of farm to observe God's plan for growing food.
- Visit a local person who may have several types of fruit trees or a vegetable garden in the yard.
- Collect seeds from the fruit snack. Plant them so children can observe their growth.

## HOW DID IT GO?

- Did this activity help children to appreciate where fruit comes from?
- Did you have moments of worship as children expressed awe and wonder at God's plan for fruit?

# Visit a Paint Store

*Children will thank God for their eyes and for a variety of colors.*

*Christian Values:* valuing God's gift of sight; praising God
*Bible:* Proverbs 20:12 (God made the hearing ear and the seeing eye.)

## MATERIALS NEEDED

permission slips
transportation and extra adults

## GETTING READY

• Arrange with the store manager the best time for the visit. Let the person know what you hope to see and what your purposes are.
• Arrange for extra transportation and parents to chaperon.

## HOW TO DO IT

• Let the children follow the manager as he or she shows the different things in the store: cans of paint, samples of different colors and shades, where paints are mixed.
• Watch how mixing two colors produces a different color, and how adding white to any color changes the shade.

## VARIATIONS

• *For younger children:* Let them explore mixing different colors by using water and food coloring or tempera paints.
• Let children enjoy looking through a kaleidoscope on your wonder table.

## HOW DID IT GO?

• How did the children conduct themselves during the trip?
• How will you follow up this experience in your art activities?

**SCIENCE DEVELOPMENT • SOCIAL-EMOTIONAL RELATIONSHIPS**

## MATERIALS NEEDED

 boxes
toy stuffed pets
empty pet food boxes
pet brushes
food containers
toy cash register
paper bags for purchases
pictures of people caring
 for farm animals

# Pet Store

*Children will learn about some of the animals God created and work with God in caring for pets.*

*Christian Values:* caring for God's creation; making choices; cooperating
*Bible:* Genesis 1:24-25 (God created many kinds of animals. We are to care for all of creation.)

## GETTING READY
- Cut boxes for cages and pet carriers.
- Display pictures of pets and people caring for farm animals in your room.
- Invite a parent to show how to care for a pet.

## HOW TO DO IT
- Have the parent bring a pet in a cage to show how to care for the pet. (Be aware of children with pet allergies.)
- Create a pet store with toy animals, boxes, and items for sale. Identify roles children can take, such as shopkeeper, cashier, caregiver, customer. Give them props to use.

## VARIATIONS
- *For younger children:* Invite a pet store owner or veterinarian to visit the class.
- Have the vet show how to care for animals, listen to their heart, or bandage a leg.
- Talk about how children can care for pets.
- Take a picture walk in the classroom and talk about how people care for farm animals.
- *For older children:* Take the older children to a pet store or animal clinic. See suggestions above.

## HOW DID IT GO?
- Did the children show they understood today's lesson? Did they care properly for their new pets?

# Picnic Echo Chant

## MATERIALS NEEDED

blanket
basket and cover
eating utensils
picnic foods
books and pictures of
  picnics

*Children will find satisfaction in working together as part of a total group activity.*

*Christian Values:* building self-esteem;
  cooperating; building community
*Bible:* Hebrews 13:16 (Help one another.)

## GETTING READY
• Find a shady, level spot to sit and spread the blanket.

## HOW TO DO IT
• Help children list their favorite activities to do when they go on a picnic.
• If picnics are unfamiliar, read or tell a story about a picnic.
• Begin the chant by saying
  "We're going on a picnic,
  and here's what we will do."
  (A child names something to do.)
  "Thank you, God, for picnics that are fun."
• All children echo teacher with each new activity mentioned.
• Say or sing your grace.

## VARIATIONS
• *For younger children:* Keep coversation of picnic activities short or stop when attention lessens.
• *For older children:* Play a "What's Missing?" game. Show children some picnic items in a basket. Cover the basket and have the children recall what they saw. Pull out items as children name them.
• Add imitative motions with the chant, if desired.

## HOW DID IT GO?
• Were children able to listen and echo the chant?
• Which children could recall the items in the basket? Which ones need more practice?

**Ages 4–6**

# Pizza Parlor

### MATERIALS NEEDED

*Children will enjoy participating in making a pizza at a pizza parlor.*

**Christian Values:** working together to serve others and God
**Bible:** Romans 12:4-6a (God has given us gifts that can be used to help people.)

## GETTING READY

- Find a pizza parlor that will let the children put pizzas together in the kitchen. Decide on the best time to go.
- Plan time for children to eat the pizzas they make and ways to express their thanks.
- Arrange transportation, permissions, insurance, and extra adult help.

## HOW TO DO IT

- At the pizza parlor divide children into groups. Have only a few in the cooking area at one time.
- The pizza chef will show the children how the dough is shaped. Then the children can assist with the toppings.

## VARIATIONS

- *For younger children:* Use the family living center to pretend to work in a pizza parlor. Find more ideas on pages 57 and 144.
- *For older children:* Use the field trip for an emphasis on the letter *P*. Think of other words that begin with *P*.
- Plan ways to reinforce the visit such as by retelling the story or sequencing the experiences.

## HOW DID IT GO?

- Were the children able to wait patiently for their turn?
- In what ways did this experience add to the child's experiential learning?

# Recycle Center

### MATERIALS NEEDED

bags for recyclables
caps or hats

*Children will become aware of recycling as a way to care for God's world.*

*Christian Values:* respecting God's world; making choices; learning responsible stewardship
*Bible:* Genesis 1:28 (People are to care for God's world.)

## GETTING READY
- Contact recycling center for information on collecting and depositing recyclable items.
- Set up space and containers for collection.
- Inform parents of project.

## HOW TO DO IT
- Encourage each child to bring in recyclable items each day for a week.
- Point out clues such as the recycle triangle symbol on items.
- Let the children take turns wearing caps and being the workers who put the items in the correct bag.

## VARIATIONS
- *For younger children:* Take the children to the kitchen at the church or preschool and ask the helpers to save recyclable items for them. Return in a week to pick them up.

- *For older children:* Sort clean, nonbreakable containers such as cereal boxes, plastic milk cartons, and aluminum cans into bags.
- Invite parents to help you by collecting recyclables in the neighborhood.

## HOW DID IT GO?
- What technique helped children remember to bring an item from home?
- Did children show an awareness of the concept of reuse or recycle?

**THINKING SKILLS • SOCIAL STUDIES READINESS**

## MATERIALS NEEDED

transportation
permission slips
instruments such as an
  electric keyboard, guitar,
  or autoharp
rhythm instruments

# Visit a School Band

*Children will begin to appreciate that musicians are helpers as they visit a band.*

*Christian Values:* appreciating and valuing others; using God's gifts for others
*Bible:* Romans 12:4-7 (God gave people different gifts that can be used to help others.)

## GETTING READY

- Request the band director to let your class visit during rehearsal. Ask if the band could play some tunes familiar to the children. Suggest that children could hear each instrument played individually.
- Gather rhythm band and other instruments.

## HOW TO DO IT

- Prepare children for the trip by discussing purposes, safety rules, and behavior.
- Talk about ways music helps people (rest, fun, dancing, worship, movies).
- Have the band director talk to the children, naming the instruments and asking a band member to play the instrument.
- Let the children play their rhythm instruments as the band plays.

## VARIATIONS

- *For younger children:* Ask someone who plays an instrument to visit with the children. Suggest some of the children's favorite songs for the person to accompany as the children sing.
- *For older children:* If the instrument is not too delicate for the children to handle, ask the visitor if the children could "play" it.
- Bring an electronic keyboard, a guitar, or an autoharp for the children to play.

## HOW DID IT GO?

- How did the children respond to the music the band played?
- What ways are there in the community for children to hear good music?

**MUSIC • THINKING SKILLS**

# Basket or Bag Story

*Children will make up or listen to a story using words that begin with the letter B.*

*Christian Values:* developing God's gift of language; working together
*Bible:* Ephesians 4:15 (We are to grow up in every way.)

## MATERIALS NEEDED

a basket or bag
small objects beginning with the letter *B* such as a block, bottle, button, baby doll, boat, bear, banana, beanbag
chart paper
marker

## GETTING READY
- Place items in the basket or bag.
- Prepare a place for writing down the children's story.

## HOW TO DO IT
- Introduce the letter *B* and the sound it makes.
- Tell the children that you have a basket (bag) of objects that begin with the letter B. Help them name all the items, making sure they begin with B.
- Say: "Today we will 'write' a silly story using these words."
- Start the story: "Once upon a time a boy had a bear." (Hold up the bear.) Children take turns adding to the story using all the objects in the basket.
- Record the story on chart paper so the children can "read" it or hear it again.

## VARIATIONS
- *For younger children:* Use the objects in a basket to tell your own story. Hold up each object as you say the name. Then tell the story just for fun.
- *For older children:* Write another story by adding objects to the basket that do not begin with the same letter. Children are to identify the *B* objects.
- Use other consonant objects such as *W* objects in a wagon and *J* objects in a jar to write a new story.

## HOW DID IT GO?
- What evidence did the children show that they can identify the letter *B* and its sound?
- Could the children build on each other's sentences even if it was silly?

**LANGUAGE DEVELOPMENT • THINKING SKILLS**

## MATERIALS NEEDED

Bible or leaflets
space for the group to sit
    together
flannelboard
figures for the
    flannelboard

# Flannelboard Story

*Children will learn a Bible story by hearing and seeing a picture story.*

*Christian Values:* learning our Christian
    heritage; developing listening skills
*Bible:* Deuteronomy 6:4-7 (Teach your children
    to love God.)

## GETTING READY

- Look through noncurrent curriculum leaflets and packet books for a story and figures.
- Practice the story so that you can tell it without a book.
- Prepare the storytelling figures for the flannelboard.

## HOW TO DO IT

- Gather the children in a comfortable place.
- Tell the story, adding the appropriate flannelboard figure as each character enters the story.
- Talk with the children about the story after you have told it.

## VARIATIONS

- *For younger children:* Tell the story to interested children and let a child add the figures to the flannelboard.
- *For older children:* Let one or two children use the flannelboard figures as they retell the story.

## HOW DID IT GO?

- In what ways can children recall the story and retell it?
- Were the flannelboard figures helpful in holding the children's interest in learning the Bible story?

**LANGUAGE DEVELOPMENT • THINKING SKILLS**

# Hand Talk

**MATERIALS NEEDED**

*Children will become aware of body movements that send messages to other people.*

**Christian Values:** learning to understand others; valuing other persons
**Bible:** Psalm 122:1 (I was glad when they said to me, "Let us go into God's house.")

## GETTING READY

- Plan a story to tell about going to church or into the church sanctuary.
- Write down parts of the story that could be emphasized by hand gestures:
    We **turn** the knob on the **big** door and **pull** it **open**. Then we **close** the door **quietly**. We see the great **big** cross on the wall and a very **little** cross on the **book** of songs.

## HOW TO DO IT

- Take children on a visit to the sanctuary. When you return, tell a story about the trip. Use hand motions when possible, and encourage children to do the motions as you retell the story.
- Retell the story and leave out some words—using only hand signs. Let children say the missing word.

## VARIATIONS

- *For younger children:* Use similar, common hand gestures to tell a story with the children about other familiar activities such as going for a walk around the schoolyard or a walk around the block.
- *For older children:* Learn to use sign language as you sing a song. Say: "When people cannot hear, they talk and sing with their hands."

## HOW DID IT GO?

- Which hand signals did children understand first? Which did they have difficulty with?

## MATERIALS NEEDED

figures from used leaflets
   or packets
metal cabinet
magnetic strips
construction paper
scissors

# Magnetic Board Stories

*Children will learn about God by listening to a Bible story and seeing it acted out.*

**Christian Values:** remembering our Christian heritage; learning through the senses
**Bible:** Deuteronomy 6:4-7 (Teach the children about our faith.)

## GETTING READY

- Choose a story and figures from used curriculum. Cut out the figures and put pieces of magnetic strips on the back of each one.
- Learn the story and practice using the figures as you tell the story.
- Glue construction paper on a convenient area of a metal cabinet for a background for your magnetic board.

## HOW TO DO IT

- Gather the children in a circle around the board.
- As you tell the story, place the appropriate magnetic figures on the board.

## VARIATIONS

- Tape the figures on craft sticks and use as stick puppets to tell the story.
- Make a story board by covering a cookie sheet with burlap or other coarse material. Glue a small piece of Velcro (the hook side) to the backs of the puppets and attach to the board.
- Puppets and magnetic figures can be left in the reading corner for the children to use.

## HOW DID IT GO?

- Did the figures hold the children's interest?
- Were the children free to use the magnetic board and figures?

# Microphone Talk

*Children will express themselves in words and respond to simple questions.*

*Christian Values:* enhancing self-esteem; affirming own growth; praising God
*Bible:* Ephesians 4:15 (We must grow in every way.)

## MATERIALS NEEDED

sturdy paper-towel tube
aluminum foil
black cloth
rubber bands

## GETTING READY

• Make a microphone by covering a cardboard tube with aluminum foil. Cut a 6-inch square from black cloth and wrap it over the top of the microphone. Hold it in place with a rubber band.

## HOW TO DO IT

• Speak into the microphone to ask a child one question at a time: "What is something you do at home to help your family?" "Who helped you get ready for school today?"
• Let the child respond using the microphone. Do not pressure shy children to talk.

## VARIATIONS

• *For older children:* Do a "Person on the street" interview with individual children to ask their opinion about community issues: "Have you seen empty cans thrown in the street? What can children do to help keep our world clean?" Make a list of questions beforehand to ask the children. Be sensitive to their answers, which may pose new questions.
• Let older children pretend to be newscasters and tell classmates what news is happening in their school, town, or family.

## HOW DID IT GO?

• Did the microphone encourage language and better listening habits?

## MATERIALS NEEDED

pictures of characters and
scenery from several
familiar storybooks:
animals, people, forest,
houses, rivers
flannelboard or newsprint
markers
tape recorder

# Mixed-up Stories

*Children will develop skills of listening, recalling, and classifying events by hearing a mixed-up story.*

*Christian Values:* using God's gifts of creativity and memory
*Bible:* Psalm 92:1 (It is good to give thanks to God.)

## GETTING READY
• Cut pictures from several favorite storybooks.

## HOW TO DO IT
• Make up a story using characters and settings from different stories. For example: "One day, Harry the Dirty Dog went into the woods. He saw a pretty gingerbread house . . . "
• Hold up the pictures or use them on a flannelboard as the story is told.
• Let the children finish it.

## VARIATIONS
• Ask a parent or friend to draw pictures for you as you tell the story.
• Record the story on a tape recorder or write it on chart paper. Listen to it again.

## HOW DID IT GO?
• Did the children have fun making up stories? Could they recall the characters and the stories from which they came?

# Participation Stories

*Children will learn and enjoy a story by participating in its telling.*

*Christian Values:* appreciating God's plan for learning; developing the gift of creativity
*Bible:* Ephesians 4:15 (We are to grow up in every way.)

**MATERIALS NEEDED**

stories with many repetitive sentences, or questions that children can answer with the help of pictures

## GETTING READY

- Become very familiar with the story and the pictures.
- Practice telling the story out loud so that you will have eye contact with the children.

## HOW TO DO IT

- Tell the story to the children using the picture book.
- Explain how you want them to help you tell the story. Say: "When I tell the story the second time, I want you to 'read' some of the lines. Each time I say 'The dog said,' I want you to say 'Bow-wow-wow.' "

## VARIATIONS

- *For younger children:* Use a story that has a lot of movement. Let the children pantomime the movements each time they appear in the story, such as "He stood up" or "She stirred harder."
- Good books for storytelling are *Rain Makes Applesauce,* by Julian Scheer; *Brown Bear, Brown Bear, What Do You See?* by Bill Martin, Jr.; *The Very Hungry Caterpillar,* by Eric Carle.

## HOW DID IT GO?

- How much did the children participate in the telling of the stories?
- Do you hear them repeat some of the sentences heard in the stories?

## MATERIALS NEEDED

any book to read aloud
12- by 15-inch newsprint
crayons, markers, or
   watercolor paints
stapler or paper punch
yarn

# Retelling With Art

*Children will illustrate their memories of the story.*

*Christian Values:* using God's gift of creativity; learning to share with others
*Bible:* 1 Corinthians 3:9 (We are workers with God.)

## GETTING READY
• Practice telling the story aloud using lots of expression or gestures.

## HOW TO DO IT
• Read a story or book aloud to the class.
• After the story, review the events that happened. Ask: "What happened first?" "What happened next?" "What happened last?"
• Give out art materials and ask children to draw something that they remember from the story. They can draw a favorite character or their favorite event.
• After everyone is finished, allow children to show their creations and talk about them. Display the art in the classroom.

## VARIATIONS
• Compile the art into one large "big book" that children can look at again and again to retell the story in their own words.

## HOW DID IT GO?
• Were some children reluctant to re-create something from the story?
• How can you encourage their creativity?

# Sing a Story

**MATERIALS NEEDED**

stories that include
singing

*Children will develop listening skills and enjoy a story by hearing it sung.*

**Christian Values:** appreciating gifts of others; developing learning skills
**Bible:** Romans 12:4-7 (God has given each of us different gifts.)

## GETTING READY
- Ask your librarian to recommend books.
- Practice singing the song. Many books include a cassette tape.

## HOW TO DO IT
- Gather the children around you and read the story. Then say: "Another way to tell this story is to sing it."
- Turn the pages to show the pictures as you sing the story or play the tape.

## VARIATIONS
- *For younger children:* Play musical recordings of Mother Goose rhymes, especially those with definite story lines. Show the pictures.
- *For older children:* Some stories use repeating refrains that the children can sing with you as you narrate the story.
- A good book to be sung is *The Little Drummer Boy*, by Katherine Davis.

## HOW DID IT GO?
- Did the children try to sing with you?
- Play the story often so the children will learn to sing it from memory.

## MATERIALS NEEDED

shallow box (12 by 18
  by 2)
story and figures from
  used leaflets or packets
light tagboard
cardboard tubes
paints
brush
scissors
glue

# Story Box

*Children will listen to a Bible story.*

*Christian Values:* remembering our Christian
  heritage; developing creativity
*Bible:* Deuteronomy 6:4-7 (Teach the children
  about our faith.)

## GETTING READY
- Choose a story from used leaflets or
  packets.
- Mount the figures on light tagboard.
- Cut the tubes into 2-inch lengths and glue
  puppets to it at the base.

## HOW TO DO IT
- Paint the inside of the shallow box with a
  light blue sky and green or brown earth.
- Stand the box on its long side and use it
  as the backdrop. As you tell the story,
  arrange the figures in front of the box like
  a diorama.
- Encourage the children to retell the story
  or make up their own story using the
  figures.
- At the end of the activity store the figures
  in the box ready for another day. Add
  figures for each new story.

## VARIATIONS
- Leave the story box in the book center for
  the children to use.

## HOW DID IT GO?
- How much of the story did the children
  remember?
- How much imagination did they show in
  using the figures on their own?

**LANGUAGE DEVELOPMENT • THINKING SKILLS**

# Stories With Sound Effects

*Children will participate in storytelling by making sound effects.*

**Christian Values:** appreciating God's plan for learning; being creative

**Bible:** Romans 12:4-7 (God has given each of us different gifts.)

## MATERIALS NEEDED

stories with a lot of sounds, such as *Roar and More*, by Karla Kuskin; *Peace at Last*, by Jill Murphy
objects and rhythm instruments to make the sounds

## GETTING READY
• Select a story that contains a lot of different sounds.

## HOW TO DO IT
• Explain how you will tell the story and what the children will do. Ask them to pay special attention to the sounds.
• Say a word from the story and discuss the sounds needed. Let the children help decide how to make each sound and which object, instrument, or voice sound might be used.
• Read the story again and let the children make the sounds each time they are called for in the story.

## VARIATIONS
• Use the sound story with a few children at a time in the reading corner.
• *For older children:* Read the story and ask the children to identify words that would be enhanced by using sounds. They can also choose the best way to make the sounds.
• Tape record the story after the children have learned it with the sounds. Enjoy listening to "their story" often.

## HOW DID IT GO?
• Did making the sounds help the children pay attention to the story?
• How many words or story characters were they able to identify by their sounds?

## MATERIALS NEEDED

parents or volunteers to come as a story character once a month
favorite books or stories
extra props to use with story

# Storybook Friend

*Children will learn listening skills and enjoyment of stories by hearing a story character read a storybook.*

*Christian Values:* sharing one's talents; showing appreciation for the gift of storytelling
*Bible:* Psalm 9:1-2 (I will give thanks. I will be glad.)

## GETTING READY

- Meet with interested parents to set up a "storybook friend" time each month. The volunteer picks a favorite story to tell to the class. On a special day the friend will come dressed as a story character or with props to use in telling the story.
- Examples: gardening tools for the Peter Rabbit story, dress like an engineer for train stories, bring in honey for Winnie the Pooh stories.

## HOW TO DO IT

- Review good listening rules with the children.
- Arrange children for Together Time.
- Listen to storyteller.
- Allow children to ask questions about the story after it has been read or told.

## VARIATIONS

- Suggest that parents donate favorite books to your library for storytelling time.

## HOW DID IT GO?

- Did the storybook friend spark a new and different interest in the storybook?

# Bible Drama

Children will learn how to experience the feelings and messages of a story.

**Christian Values:** accepting all persons; remembering our heritage
**Bible:** Romans 12:4-7 (We have different gifts to use for the good of the community.)

## MATERIALS NEEDED

Bible

## GETTING READY
- Select and mark age-appropriate Bible verses and stories that can be dramatized. Examples are
    1 John 3:18 or Ephesians 4:32—Our love should not be just words. (*Let children act out ways to show love.*)
    Mark 11:1-10—Jesus entered Jerusalem on Palm Sunday. (*What might we do when we are afraid? excited?*)
- Choose favorite storybooks of the children that include feelings, actions, and familiar customs.

## HOW TO DO IT
- Open the Bible or storybook and read one selected verse or story. Talk about its meaning to the person in the story. Ask the children how they would feel or what they would have done.
- Let the children act out the message or the feelings that the person had.

## VARIATIONS
- Share dramatizations with other classes.

## HOW DID IT GO?
- Were children able to show examples of feelings or behaviors?

**SOCIAL-EMOTIONAL RELATIONSHIPS • THINKING SKILLS**

# Box Theater

## MATERIALS NEEDED

small box with lid
small objects such as toys
nature objects

*Children will use their imagination as they listen to, watch, and participate in a story.*

*Christian Values:* developing God's gifts of imagination and creativity
*Bible:* Genesis 1:26-28 (God created people with the ability to think and learn.)

## GETTING READY

- Put the items in the box.
- Gather the children. Put the box where it is visible to everybody.

## HOW TO DO IT

- Shake the box and ask the children to guess what is inside.
- Take the objects out and talk about their texture, shape, name, and so on.
- Each day make up stories to go with the contents. For example: "This leaf was blown off the branch of the maple tree. It landed on my back screen door. I didn't hear a sound. What do you think happened?"
- Let children add their ideas or make up their own stories.
- Later, use the box theater and contents to tell familiar stories.

## VARIATIONS

- Leave the box theater in the room for a learning center.
- Encourage the children to contribute objects and stories for the theater.

## HOW DID IT GO?

- How did the children relate to the activity creatively?
- Which children used the box theater on their own?

# Talking a Story

## MATERIALS NEEDED

favorite storybooks
tape recorder

*Children will enjoy retelling a story and sharing it with others by recording it.*

**Christian Values:** using minds to think; giving love by sharing talents with others
**Bible:** Psalm 139:13a (God created every part of me.)

## GETTING READY
- Set up a small table or space on the floor with a tape recorder and several books that are familiar to the children.
- Train children to use the tape recorder. Use colored circles taped on the buttons: green for play, yellow for rewind, red for stop, orange for record.

## HOW TO DO IT
- Allow each child to use the tape recorder to "read" one of the books in his or her own words.
- This can be demonstrated in a Together Time activity and used as an open center during the year.
- Allow the child to listen to the recording and to share it with others.

## VARIATIONS
- All of the stories can be saved and used for a listening activity.
- Send taped stories home to share with parents.
- Use a VCR camera to film children retelling a story.

## HOW DID IT GO?
- Were the children happy to hear their own voices telling the story?

**LANGUAGE DEVELOPMENT • THINKING SKILLS**

## MATERIALS NEEDED

½ sheet of posterboard for
  each character
paper punch
yarn
markers or oil pastel
  colors

# Character Cards

*Children will gain self-confidence by dramatically reciting character parts with placard cards.*

***Christian Values:*** enhancing self-esteem; overcoming fear
***Bible:*** Matthew 9:35 (Jesus went about teaching and preaching.)

## GETTING READY
• Select a story in which the characters say the same lines repeatedly.

## HOW TO DO IT
• Cut posterboard in half.
• On each card draw and color a picture of one of the story characters.
• Punch two holes in the top of the card. Thread the yarn through and tie around a child's neck.
• Children will say the lines of their character while the teacher serves as narrator.
• With animal characters use the animal sounds and expression in their voices.

## VARIATIONS
• Find an artistic person to illustrate the character cards. Use markers to color pictures.
• Laminate the cards to use again.

## HOW DID IT GO?
• Did the children enjoy roleplaying the characters?
• How did the children show their self-confidence in getting up before their classmates?

# Classifying Seasonal Words

*Children will enrich their language skills by associating words with God's plan for seasons.*

**Christian Values:** enhancing self-esteem; developing expressive language
**Bible:** Genesis 8:22 (God promises the continuance of spring and fall, summer and winter.)

## MATERIALS NEEDED

construction paper
marker
art supplies for
  appropriate seasonal
  background

## GETTING READY
- Cut 2- by 6-inch word strips from construction paper.
- Make seasonal backgrounds for the bulletin board. Write the name of a season at the top and add one of the following:
    *Fall*—finger-painted leaf shapes
    *Winter*—snowflakes
    *Spring*—a mural of spring flowers
    *Summer*—sailboats

## HOW TO DO IT
- Children brainstorm words to associate with the current season.
- Record words on word strips and display on a seasonal background. Examples:
*Fall*—colors, leaves, cool, rakes, sweaters;
*Winter*—cold, snow, ice, mittens, sled;
*Spring*—flowers, baby animals, green grass;
*Summer*—hot, swim, sunny, vacation.

## VARIATIONS
- *For younger children:* Say a word and let the children tell you the season.

- *For older children:* Write a group story using words the children associate with this season.
- Write a simple thanksgiving prayer or seasonal litany to use in worship.

## HOW DID IT GO?
- Were you able to challenge the children to think of new words to associate with the season?

## MATERIALS NEEDED

familiar stories or nursery rhymes

# Do You Remember?

*Children will use their memory and imagination skills to recall stories they have heard.*

*Christian Values:* developing thinking abilities; developing imaginations

*Bible:* Hebrews 13:16 (Do good and share.)

## GETTING READY

- Prepare a list of questions about characters in familiar stories. For example: "Who wore a red cape and hood and got lost in the woods?" "Who sat down and saw a spider?"
- Make a cozy storytelling place.

## HOW TO DO IT

- Ask children for their favorite stories.
- Prepare a list of questions to help children recall the characters or events in the stories.
- Tell the story or read the nursery rhyme after the question is answered.

## VARIATIONS

- *For younger children:* They may need more hints or use pictures when trying to recall stories.

- *For older children:* Extend the activity by asking "what if" questions. "What if Little Red Riding Hood had worn blue?" "What if the three bears had been eating a ham sandwich?"

## HOW DID IT GO?

- Did this activity spark an interest in wanting to hear stories and rhymes again?

# Story Sequencing

*Children will develop their listening and memory skills by illustrating a story in sequence.*

*Christian Values:* developing minds; using creativity

*Bible:* Genesis 1:27 (God created us with many talents.)

## MATERIALS NEEDED

any story or storybook
8½-by-11 white paper, one
   sheet per child
crayons or markers

## GETTING READY
- Fold papers in half, then in half again.
- Unfold so that there are four boxes on the paper. Number the squares.
- Practice telling the story.

## HOW TO DO IT
- Tell or read the story to the class.
- Ask children: "What happened first in the story?" (Encourage all appropriate answers.)
- Continue until there are four major events that can be recalled.
- Instruct children to use crayons and paper to illustrate these four events.

## VARIATIONS
- Have the teacher demonstrate on the chalkboard where to draw the four pictures from the story.
- Let children retell the story by "reading" their paper.

## HOW DID IT GO?
- Which children had difficulty in remembering the story as they did their illustrations? How can you help these children?

# Noah's Ark

## MATERIALS NEEDED

paper bags
pairs of animal figures
large toy boat
Bible, or a storybook of
Noah

*Children will be able to help tell a Bible story.*

*Christian Values:* remembering our Christian
heritage; developing God's gifts
*Bible:* Genesis 1:25 (God made all kinds of
animals on the earth.)

## GETTING READY

• Put one animal from each pair in a
separate paper bag. Stand the other
animal of each pair in a line going into
the boat.

## HOW TO DO IT

• Tell the story of Noah at the age level you
teach.
• When the story describes Noah putting
pairs of animals on the ark, let each child
come up, select a bag, pull out the
animal, and name it. Place it beside the
matching animal in the line to the ark.
• When all animal pairs are in line, finish
telling the story.

## VARIATIONS

• Have a storyteller dress up as Noah to tell
his own personal story.
• After the story, cover the animals with a
cloth and see how many the children can
recall or describe.

## HOW DID IT GO?

• Was the story of Noah familiar to any of
the children?
• Were there any animals that the children
could not recognize?

**LANGUAGE DEVELOPMENT • SCIENCE DEVELOPMENT**

# A Philippine Legend

*Children will learn to appreciate traditions of other countries by hearing a story from the Philippines.*

**Christian Values:** valuing others and their culture
**Bible:** Genesis 1:26 (Each person is created special by God.)

## MATERIALS NEEDED

flannelboard figures of two moths—one larger than the other
lighted candle

## GETTING READY
- Tell the children that this story comes from the Philippine Islands.
- Become familiar with the story and practice telling it with animation.

## HOW TO DO IT
- Sit in a circle with a lighted candle in the center. Say: "Today we will hear a story from the Philippine Islands."

### Baby Moth
Mother Moth warned Baby Moth, "Don't fly near that candle. You'll be burned." At that Mother Moth flew away.

Baby Moth looked at the beautiful flame. She flew around it; nearer and nearer she came to it. "It's just pleasantly warm," she thought. So she flew closer and closer. "Ouch!" she cried, as the flame burned the tip of her wing.

## VARIATIONS
- Lengthen the story by giving Baby Moth a few more thoughts or more conversation with Mother Moth.
- Give the children an opportunity to retell the story by using flannelboard figures to tell the story.
- *For older children:* Tape or glue each paper moth onto the end of a string. Act out the story by letting two children run around the circle waving the string up and down so the moths will fly as the story is told.

## HOW DID IT GO?
- How did the children react to the story?
- Can any of the children retell the story?

**SCIENCE DEVELOPMENT • SOCIAL STUDIES READINESS**

## MATERIALS NEEDED

3-by-5 index cards
pictures for your story
glue stick
markers

# Oral Rebus Stories

*Children will participate orally in a story by using cue cards for sounds and words.*

*Christian Values:* enhancing self-esteem; developing language potential
*Bible:* Luke 2:40 (Jesus grew and was filled with wisdom.)

## GETTING READY
- Select a story in which the same animal sounds and characters are repeated.
- Find magazine pictures or draw pictures of the objects needed and glue them to index cards.

## HOW TO DO IT
- Help the children determine the sounds or words that will be used whenever each card is seen.
- Tell the story, holding up the appropriate cue card for the children's response.
- In the following example the cue cards are boldface. "Bessie says we should drink **three** cups of **milk** each day to make our **bones** strong. '**Moo-Moo**,' says Bessie."

## VARIATIONS
- *For younger children:* Glue pieces of felt to make pictures for children to touch.
- Use this technique in telling Bible stories.
- Use cue cards to emphasize factual content you want the children to repeat.

## HOW DID IT GO?
- Were the children attentive today?
- Were there other cards you could have made to fit the story?

# Experience a Poem

*Children will express their interpretation of a poem in visual art.*

*Christian Values:* discovering and developing our gift of creativity
*Bible:* Genesis 1:27 (God created us with many talents.)

## MATERIALS NEEDED

drawing paper
crayons, markers
construction paper
chart paper

## GETTING READY
• Gather supplies.
• Select a short simple poem about nature that has concrete visual images and is filled with action.
• Print the poem in manuscript on chart paper.

## HOW TO DO IT
• Have children listen as you read the poem to them.
• Tell children to close their eyes and try to see in their minds a picture of what is happening. Tell them to think about the colors they see, and how the poem makes them feel.
• Give each child paper and crayons. Ask the children to draw a picture to go with the poem.

## VARIATIONS
• *For younger children:* The experience of expression is more important than the drawing. Many children this age will not be able to draw realistically and may not be able to tell you what the picture is.
• *For older children:* Type the poem in the center of a sheet of paper. Leave room for the children to draw around the poem.
• Select a poem that can be interpreted with creative movement such as butterflies moving in the wind.

## HOW DID IT GO?
• Were the children able to verbally and visually interpret the poem?
• What would have increased their participation?

## MATERIALS NEEDED

a clown puppet or
materials for making
puppet (white, red, and
black felt; ruffle; yarn;
tempera paint)
stories about solving
conflicts

# Problem-solver Puppet

*Children will learn about problem solving by talking it through with a puppet or hearing the puppet tell a story.*

***Christian Values:*** valuing others; living together
in love
***Bible:*** Romans 12:10 (Love one another.)

## GETTING READY

• Buy or make a clown puppet. Cut out two felt mitten shapes with a thumb on each side. Sew sides together. Add yarn hair. Cut some funny ears, a happy mouth, and large eyes. Glue in place. Sew a ruffle at the neck. Add bright colors of paint.

## HOW TO DO IT

• Use the clown for solving conflicts such as grabbing toys. When a child has a problem, sit with the child and have the clown tell the story.
• Encourage the child to converse with the clown as questions are asked that help the child resolve his or her own problem.
• Use stories that do not moralize, scold, punish, or give a pat answer. End on a happy note of laughter, a hug, or an apology.

## VARIATIONS

• *For younger children:* Let the puppet sing some songs about playing kindly or being cooperative and sharing.
• *For older children:* Use two puppets. Let the children roleplay the incident and try to discover ways to resolve the problem.
• Let two children not involved in the conflict roleplay the problem scene and suggest a possible way to resolve the conflict.

## HOW DID IT GO?

• Which stories did the children respond to best? Plan to use them again.
• What evidence was there that children solved their problems more peaceably?

# Our Book

## MATERIALS NEEDED

large sheets of newsprint
felt-tip marker
glue
old magazines
children's scissors
crayons or markers
colored construction paper
stapler and staples

*Children will develop God's gift of communication and affirm each child's personal story by making a class book.*

**Christian Values:** making choices; cooperating
**Bible:** 1 Peter 5:7 (God cares about you.)

## GETTING READY
• Tape large sheets of newsprint on the wall at the children's eye level.

## HOW TO DO IT
• Suggest topics for a book to be written by the children. Topics might be school friends, spring, family, or a celebration.
• Have each child tell a story while the teacher records the story on the newsprint.
• Let the children illustrate ideas by cutting and gluing magazine pictures. Older children may draw and color their own illustrations.
• Assemble all of the pages and staple the book between two pages of colored construction paper.
• Reread the book often to the children.

## VARIATIONS
• *For younger children:* Select appropriate precut pictures and tell a story about each one.
• Invite the parents to come and read the class book.
• *For older children:* Invite another class to see your book. Let the children help "read" the story to their guests.

## HOW DID IT GO?
• Did children have trouble expressing their own ideas in story form?
• Did children suggest topics for another class book?

# Learning Through Centers

The concept of teaching by centers, of letting children make choices among activities, and of letting them move to new activities as their interest changes, is a difficult concept for some adults to use.

*Young children learn best through short concrete experiences. Allowing children to move among planned learning activities capitalizes on the way that they learn best.*

If the curriculum calls for the children to learn about plants and how they grow, the teacher should plan self-directed activities in as many centers as possible that would help the children learn something about the growth of plants.

**Science Center:** Children might "plant" lima beans in plastic zipper bags and hang them in a sunny window.

**Home Living Center:** Children might rinse mung beans to make bean sprouts.

**Creative Arts Center:** Children could make leaf rubbings of different sizes and shapes.

**Building Center:** Children might build a farm and pretend to plant crops.

**Book Center:** Children could look at many books about plants and how they grow.

**Music Center:** Children might sing songs about plants.

**Values of Learning Centers**
- Children learn to be self-directed.
- Children have opportunities to make choices and to live with the consequences of those choices.
- Children learn independence and self-reliance. They learn many things about their preferences and abilities.
- Children learn how to set goals and plan for themselves.
- They learn self-reliance.
- They grow as God has planned for them to do.

*This approach of offering several activities assumes that children learn in different ways and allows each child to concentrate on ways that appeal most to him or her.*

# How to Get From Here to There

One of the most important and mysterious things that a teacher does with a group of children is to help them move from one activity to another. If transitions are not handled skillfully, chaos can result.

Young children cannot end center time, clean up, and move to together time without direction. Children need a warning that center time will end soon. When clean-up time arrives, the teacher can sing a "clean-up" song. The children will recognize the usual song and will begin to clean up on their own. Children should be involved in cleanup, but they often need teachers to help them organize the task.

When children have finished their task and have nothing to do, they may begin to run around the room or engage in unacceptable behavior. Since there are two teachers in the room, one teacher can sit with the children who are finished and involve them in reading, singing, or finger games. If there is

not a second teacher in the room, the children can be taught to sit on the rug and look at a book until all the children have completed their task.

When it is time to return to the room from outdoor play, teachers should follow a similar procedure. The children should be notified, toys put away, and the children gathered together before the gate is opened. Teachers should be sure that all the children stay together as they walk back to the room. Teachers can make this a pleasant process by singing a walking song or reciting a chant in unison.

Transitional activities are helpful when some of the class members are involved in an activity such as setting the table for lunch or snack. The other children can do transitional activities or respond to the directions on musical activity records until the table is ready.

Transitions are a necessary part of group life. Smooth transitions are part of a classroom in which children are treated with acceptance and respect.

# Creative Activities

Painting, gluing, coloring, cutting and pasting, making crafts or gifts, and creating with play dough are activities one would expect to find in a classroom of young children. But have you ever thought about why these activities are used? Of what value are they to young children?

### What Will They Learn?

Some activities in this book contribute to problem-solving and thinking abilities. Other activities help develop small-muscle skills. These activities allow young children to use their hands and fingers, which improves their hand–eye coordination.

Creative activities also promote self-esteem because teachers and children can regard every attempt as successful. There is no right or wrong.

## *There need be no failure.*

Through the freedom to create, children's imaginations soar. Their sense of satisfaction is guaranteed because they are free to try again. When creative activities are used within a group experience, they enable children to learn to cooperate and to work together.

As you plan activities, remember that children under five years of age are just learning how to use the materials provided for creative work. The children will want to explore and discover what can be done.

## *The process is more important than the product.*

### The Role of the Teacher

Teachers should not predetermine what the children's work will look like. The teacher's role is to
1. provide a variety of materials for the activities;
2. give the children some directions (for example: "Press the sponge into the container of paint and make marks on the paper");
3. let children make their own discoveries;
4. provide children with creative activities that encourage them to stretch their imaginations, make decisions, and cooperate with others;
5. help them enjoy discovering their own unique gifts and find joy and a sense of satisfaction in using their gift of creativity.

### Freedom for You Too

Teachers gain several advantages by allowing the children to create freely. First, you do not have to be "artistic." (Whew! What a relief.) Second, you will spend less time (thank goodness!) in precutting parts of projects as well as less time instructing the children about how to do the activity. Ultimately, you are freed to observe the children's progress, to talk with them, and to encourage them in their efforts.

Giving children freedom to create does not mean you allow them to operate without some rules or boundaries. Set up the art table with places for about four children at one time. Display a "turn list" on the wall to alert *you* to whose turn is next. Direct the waiting children to choose another activity and promise to tell them when their turn comes.

Think through the steps of each activity; plan ways that the children can help themselves to the materials without much assistance. Guide the children in good work habits and the proper care and use of the art supplies.

### Help Parents Understand

Sometimes you may need to help parents understand their children's creative activities. You may need to explain that a painting is not a picture of anything; it is simply an activity appropriate for that age. Coloring is a process of experimenting with color, texture, and design. When young children are ready and able, they will draw shapes and figures on their own.

You can help the children's art efforts look more attractive to parents by choosing colors of paint and paper that look pleasing together. By using the primary colors of red, yellow, and blue, you can also ensure that paintings will look good.

### Develop God's Gift of Creativity

Creative activities are not just for the children. They are also opportunities for you as teachers and other caregivers to use your own gift of creativity. God gave human beings the capacity for creativity. You can develop it in yourself and in the children.

## *Allowing children to discover their own creativity is what is important.*

# Good Teachers Plan Weekly!

In every licensed program for children in America, teachers should be required to make weekly lesson plans. Let's look at some steps for effective planning that will help children learn.

## Begin With Your Purpose
• As your teaching team begins to prepare the session, ask yourselves some very simple but important questions:
1. Why is it important to the children to study this unit?
2. What will be our purpose?
3. What do we want the children to learn?
• Write your measurable purpose statement.
• List as many concepts as you can think of that you want the children to know at the end of the unit.
• Narrow your focus to three or four major learnings you expect the children to know.
• List the skills or attitudes or behaviors you want the children to acquire as a result of this study.

## Choose Your Activities
• Focus on activities that would help you achieve this purpose. Note each one.
• Check off any that are not appropriate for the age level. Do the children have the ability and skills to do it?
• Check off any activities that children have used recently or did not enjoy doing.
• Do you have a balance of activities that cover a variety of skills and cogitive learnings?
• Do you have enough, but not too many, activities for each day?
• Did you include active as well as quiet activities?

• Are the activities easily supervised?
• Do the activities involve children in doing and experiencing the content?

## Check Equipment and Supplies
• Make a list of equipment and supplies needed. Check to see what is on hand and what you will need to buy.
• Are the supplies within your expense budget? How many will be reusable? Do they represent good stewardship of the earth's resources?

## Plan Your Time
• Think of the time needed for each activity and determine if that activity represents the best use of the available time.

## Room Arrangement and Space
• Is your space appropriate for this activity?

## Make Teacher Assignments
• Do you have teachers who possess the skills and information needed?
• Do you have enough adults to help?
• List any preparations needed before class begins, such as mixing paint or finding teaching pictures.
• Assign a teacher responsible for each task.
   Planning is important because it helps teachers create an orderly learning environment for children. If we want children to believe that God has created an orderly world, we must have order in our classrooms. When we have order and planning, we are free to respond to the children's comments and responses and any surprising things that happen.

*Planning is important because it helps teachers create an orderly learning environment for children. If we want children to believe that God has created an orderly world, we must have order in our classrooms.*

# Guiding Children

### Appropriate Behavior
The ways teachers discipline should help children learn something. We should be teaching them self-control and appropriate behavior, not just stopping undesirable behavior or punishing them.

### Planning for Self-discipline
Teachers may unknowingly contribute to children's misbehavior by poor planning. Ask yourself the following questions:
- Am I expecting too much of the children and their abilities?
- Do the activities interest and challenge the boys and girls?
- Is the room arranged so that the children can use the materials?
- Do they have adequate space for play?
- Did I select toys and activities appropriate for the children's ages?
- Am I asking children to sit for longer periods of time than they are able?

> *We should be teaching them self-control and appropriate behavior, not just stopping undesirable behavior or punishing them.*

### Giving Directions
Listen to yourself give directions to the children. Is your voice loud? Teachers model how children should behave. If you speak loudly, the children will copy the behavior. If you speak softly, the children will also speak more quietly.

### Preparing for Transitions
Young children often resist changes in activities. Teachers can work on effective transitions in which the children are notified in advance that an activity will end. Teachers can reflect the children's feelings by comments such as "I know you wish you could play in the block center all day, but it is time to pick up the blocks now."

### Using Positive Language
Teachers can create a positive atmosphere in their classes by stating everything in a positive rather than a negative way. Say: "The play dough stays on the table" rather than "Don't take the play dough to the block center." Help the child learn what he or she should do rather than cannot do.

### Practicing Effective Guidance Methods
Effective guidance techniques preserve the self-esteem of children while teaching them how to behave better in a particular situation.

**Redirection** works with children as young as infants and as old as kindergarteners. When an infant approaches something dangerous, the easiest way to redirect the behavior is by showing the child something more interesting. Kindergarteners can also be redirected through verbal commands stated in a positive way.

**Reinforcement** is an effective technique that can be used frequently. When a child does something you like, say something positive, such as, "Thank you for picking up the blocks. That was very helpful." The child then feels good about what he or she has done and is likely to repeat that action.

Ignoring inappropriate behavior is a means of negative reinforcement that can be very effective. It is particularly effective with tantrums or clowning around.

### Avoiding Ineffective Methods
**Time-out** is a frequently used method that is not as effective as many teachers think. Many times teachers will tell a toddler or two-year-old to sit in the time-out chair and think about what he or she has done. Cognitively, children of this age are not capable of thinking about what they have done and evaluating its appropriateness.

# Learning Through Dramatic Play

A two-year-old went into the home living center, put on a hat, picked up a doll, and sat down in the rocking chair. He then put the doll in the doll bed, stirred something in a bowl in the play sink, removed his hat, and wandered off, all in a matter of minutes.

Two-year-olds benefit from dramatic play because their ability to pretend is emerging. We can help this ability develop by providing props and equipment and making suggestions of situations to pretend.

Three-year-olds will probably play beside one another and talk to each other about what they are doing. Their play lasts a little longer. They may talk to their teacher or another child about their pretend building.

Four- and five-year-olds go into a center with a plan, or develop a plan very quickly. They may name the structure they are building, such as a church or tower. In another center, one child may pick up the crying baby. Another child may be rushing off to work. The whole "family" may be preparing for a picnic.

Young children use the dramatic play centers in their classrooms according to their abilities to pretend and to engage in social play.

## Values of Dramatic Play

For young children, pretend play helps them
—learn about themselves and the world
—remember and reflect on their experiences and then to rehearse them
—think about the meanings of an experience
—try out various adult roles and gain a feeling for what that role is like
—practice relating to one another
—learn how to convince other persons to agree with their ideas
—learn the art of compromise as they work on ways to include everyone's ideas

Older children will engage in more mature, sophisticated play. They can pretend to be a parent and do what they have seen and heard parents doing. They can pretend to be a baby for a while. They can pretend to be the doctor or nurse who gives "shots." Children tend to gather in groups of three or four in each center. They have to negotiate about how the play will go, who will take what role, or who will wear what clothing.

## Role of the Teacher

1. Teachers make the dramatic play center attractive.
2. They allow plenty of time for play to unfold.
3. They provide sufficient space for children to play without crowding one another.
4. Teachers keep the center neat and orderly with places to store things easily.
5. Teachers can add props and costumes that will stimulate the creative play of children.
6. Teachers prepare storage space for the props. Props can be rotated to challenge new ideas, interest, and creativity.
7. Teachers plan experiences for the center. A play hospital, car repair shop, or an office could be set up in addition to the home living center.

> *Young children use the dramatic play centers in their classrooms according to their abilities to pretend and to engage in social play.*

## Values for Christian Education

Learning through dramatic play has religious implications. As the children play, they are working on their personal answers to life's three big questions: "Who am I?" "Who are you?" "What is the world like?"

When young children begin to get Christian answers to these questions—when they begin to think of themselves and others as valuable persons and the world as a good place to be—they can believe that their teachers, their parents, and God love them just the way they are.

# Making Math Real

Young children learn math by having experiences with objects that help them understand mathematical concepts.

## Math Reveals God's Laws

Is there a religious aspect to the study of mathematics? One might wonder how math is theological. Mathematics is a discipline that reflects the dependability and steadfastness of God and God's creation. Math facts are always the same. They do not change. We can introduce young children to mathematics in practical ways so that they come to understand math as a tool for studying God's creation rather than as a school subject that is hard to understand.

## Learning Values in Math

There are many values to be learned as preschoolers investigate meaningful math concepts. Among these values are
1. building a child's self-esteem
2. creating independence
3. gaining a sense of time
4. anticipating holidays
5. developing problem-solving skills
6. growing development of language
7. thinking and investigative skills
8. building social skills
9. developing memory skills

Many adults find math hard to understand because they did not have concrete experiences in math before they were asked to begin abstract activities using math. Young children think concretely. When they learn to count, they only memorize the sequence of the numbers. They do not have an understanding of the meaning of the numbers. Today teachers know how to provide activities that will help children discover math. Plan to use the following activities throughout the year as you give your class a sound foundation in math that is real!

| Activity | Procedure |
|---|---|
| Concept of pairs | —Children begin to understand the concept of *two* as they realize that they have two hands, two arms, two eyes, two ears, two legs.<br>—Let children group objects in pairs or complete a pattern by adding a second block or clothespin to a card. |
| Ordering objects | —Younger children can learn to order three objects from small to larger to largest.<br>—Older preschoolers can do more complicated sets of several objects. |
| Matching numbers | —Give young children a set of cards with a number of colored press-on dots on them. Children can then be asked to put the same number of clothespins on each card as there are dots on the card. |
| Sequencing | —Older preschoolers can learn sequencing when they are asked to copy a repeating pattern of blocks or dots on a card.<br>—Do a one-to-one correspondence activity by putting one of six tennis balls in each of six cups or a muffin tin. |
| Quantities | —Three- to five-year-olds can set the table by putting a cup and a napkin by each chair.<br>—They can also help divide foods by counting out fruit slices and crackers for each child. |
| Graphing | —Fours and fives can vote for their favorite color. Count their raised hands and make a graph to show how many children voted for each color.<br>—Develop a chart that shows who is present. Children mark the spaces themselves. Count the number present. |
| Correspondence | —Make paper bears and clothing for the bears from different patterns of wall paper. Let children match the clothing to the bears. |
| Calendar | —Children mark a calendar daily and see the sequence of the numbers. |
| Equations | —Use wooden cubes, craft sticks, or felt pieces to make equations. Focus on *five*. Give each child sets of five felt pieces and ask them to arrange them in as many ways as they can. They could group two pieces and three pieces, four and one, and so on. Record what they had figured out. |

# Exciting Science Activities

A science center is a very important center for preschool classrooms, even for children as young as three. Many early childhood educators feel at a loss to know how to provide hands-on activities that children will understand. A wonderful discovery awaits, however, as we learn that there are appropriate activities for children and that they are at our fingertips. Teachers may also be surprised to learn that many activities we are already doing may involve scientific processes that are not recognized.

## How to Plan

Teachers of young children need to plan activities in three major areas of the sciences: biology, chemistry, and physics.

It is good to have a place in your room reserved for science. Having a science center gives plants and animals a place to grow, and it gives you a place to set up special activities. It can also provide the children a quiet place for observation.

## Teaching Biology

*Plants and seeds:*
• Give children seeds to plant for a gift or to take home; save some to plant in the classroom.
• Keep books in the classroom about growing seeds.
• Act out and sing songs about growing seeds.
• Plant seeds in clear plastic cups where children can watch the growth process.
• Let children plant mung beans in a flat container, water them daily, and eat them in a salad. Show the children the tiny whole plants including leaves, stem, and roots that have emerged from the seed.
• Plant grass and watch it grow.
• Plan a space outside where children can have their own bed to plant flowers or vegetables.
• Save pumpkin seeds from fall to spring and plant them in the school garden. In the fall harvest your own pumpkin.
• Look for any of the following plant/seed combinations in your area: cottonwood trees with seed pods, oak tree seed pods or acorns, mulberry trees loaded with berries.

*Animals, insects, creatures:*
• Some classrooms have small animals so that children can observe the babies that are born and how both parents care for the babies.

• Silkworms are often raised in classrooms so that young children can see a whole life cycle from the hatching eggs, to the growth of the larva, to the spinning of the cocoon, and the emergence of the moths.
• Use unplanned encounters with animal life, such as ants, to lead children into discussions about how ants live and what they eat.
• Use good picture books about animals.

## Teaching Chemistry

• Mix food coloring or paints and observe what happens.
• Observe the changes when play dough is made.
• Heat margarine or cheese and observe the results.
• Watch water boil. What happens?
• Add baking powder to boiling water and see what the result is.

## Teaching Physics

*Block building:* As children learn to balance blocks or build a structure from manipulatives, they learn about *gravity* and *balance*.
*Creative art:* If you provide a marbling art activity, or just roll with marbles, children learn something about *velocity*.
*Manipulatives:* When you offer construction activities in the art center you are allowing children to experiment with *balance* and *gravity*.
*Carpentry:* Woodworking activities in which the children begin to use hammers and saws also involve basic physics such as *inclines*.
*Science center:* Toys and experiments that involve magnets introduce children to *magnetic fields*.

## Stewardship of the Earth

Christians believe that God created the universe and that it is good. Therefore we should demonstrate care and respect for all of life.
• We can teach children to observe harmless insects rather than killing them.
• We can teach children the importance of using the resources of our world wisely.

• When we give our children many experiences and teach them to have a respectful attitude toward creation, we have given them a good foundation both in science and in religion.

# Developing Language Skills

One of the most dramatic developments in the life of young children is that of language. At the end of two years, children have a rather large vocabulary, but this will vary. Children who are encouraged to speak more often will develop more language. Children who are exposed to many words in their environment will have larger vocabularies.

## What Can Teachers Do?

Classes for young children should not be silent. They should be laboratories for the development of language. If teachers are to instill a love for language and develop it to its fullest, the following suggestions may be helpful.

Teachers need to
—speak children's names often;
—use a wide variety of words for the children's benefit. Instead of using the word *upset*, for instance, the teacher could say *sad*, *disappointed*, *annoyed*, *angry*, or *concerned*.
—give opportunities for children to speak in sentences without correcting their grammar;
—provide opportunities for children to express ideas and then value the ideas;
—plan experiences that encourage children to talk to each other and to adults;
—teach rhymes, nonsense words, and basic vocabulary words;
—answer children's questions logically and truthfully.

## Encouraging Written Language

Parents and teachers have long been concerned about whether children would learn to read. Once children have developed oral language, they show more and more interest in written language through books, paper, stories, and in all places in their environment.

The learn-to-read method that is currently most popular with educators is called whole language. It is fun to use because it assumes that children will "get" reading and writing if they have many experiences with using books and are given opportunities to write. This method also assumes that children will learn to read more easily if they enjoy reading.

> *Once children have developed oral language, they show more and more interest in written language.*

## What to Do

1. Read to children individually or in small groups.
2. Use all kinds of stories and poetry.
3. Encourage children to "pour over" books that have intricate pictures and few words.
4. Let children "read the pictures" to get information and to share ideas with the adults.
5. Read large-format books to a whole group of children at once. Children see the words over and over and associate the look of the words with their sound.
6. Use books with repeating lines. In hearing a line over and over, children know what to expect next.
7. Find and tell good sequence stories and let the children try to figure out what the words mean.
8. Provide opportunities to write down the children's own ideas and experiences to help them understand that writing is talking on paper.
9. Encourage children to dictate stories that the teacher will write.
10. Make booklets of stories written and illustrated by children to use in your own library.

Young children also write stories that are fun and that reflect their feelings. They enjoy scribbling on paper and then telling an adult what that writing "says." The whole language approach recognizes the child's attempt to communicate by asking the child to tell what he or she has written. If the child prefers, the adult can write the words above the scribbles so that everyone will be able to understand the writing. This approach to reading encourages children to enjoy reading and writing as a lifelong skill. It encourages them to use symbols to communicate ideas and to enjoy sharing them.

# The Why and How of Field Trips

Planning field trips for classes of children is exciting. Going away from the school or center offers a change of routine and scenery that is appealing.

In planning field trips for young children, it is always important to consider the reason or purpose for the trip and whether it is appropriate for the age level. In an educational setting everything we do should support one of our goals for the program.

### Evaluating Field Trip Possibilities

There are many factors to consider in planning field trips with young children. You may find the following guidelines helpful.

Will this experience be appropriate to the children's developmental level? Young children do not stand and listen well for very long. Will the proposed trip take the children into an environment where they can move, or will they be expected to listen for longer than three to five minutes at a time?

Will children learn by doing, touching, and interacting with materials? Young children live in the present and have little understanding of the past or the future. Trips to most historical sites or parks, therefore, would not be that meaningful to young children.

Will the nature of the presentation by the tour leader be appropriate? A trip to the post office would be more interesting if it included weighing a letter, buying the stamps, and dropping the letter in the mail slot. Stamping the letter with a post mark and noting the date would be fun and a learning experience.

Will the conditions be safe and not frightening to young children? Will there be loud noises or other situations that might frighten the children so much that they would not learn anything?

Will the travel time be too long? Young children should not be expected to sit still in a vehicle for more than twenty to thirty minutes. If teachers and children are exhausted when they arrive, they do not learn very much or enjoy themselves at the site of the field trip.

Will one of the teachers go to the site before the class goes? Taking the time to visit the site of a proposed field trip helps the teacher know the trip is age-appropriate. The teacher also then knows how to reach the site and how long it will take to get there.

Will you have enough adults on the trip **to supervise the children adequately?** It is important to have an adult in each vehicle in addition to the driver. The driver should be able to concentrate on driving and the other adult can relate to the children. The number of adults needed varies with the age level.

### Possible Field Trips

*Two-year-olds:* Twos should be taken on a minimum of short, safe field trips:
• an outing to the park to play or to feed the ducks;
• a walk in the neighborhood to see flowers;
• a trip to stand near the corner to watch cars and trucks go by as the traffic light changes;
• a trip to the corner mailbox to mail a letter.

*Three-year-olds:* Field trips should be calm and simple:
• a visit to the veterinarian's office when the class pet needs a checkup;
• a visit to a friendly dentist who will count teeth, squirt water into mouths, and give out toothbrushes;
• a trip to a nearby farmers market to buy fruit for snacks.

*Four-year-olds:* Fours can handle more complex trips such as
• going to the fire station
• visiting the zoo
• discovering a farm

*Five-year-olds:* Fives like more technical trips such as
• a trip to the natural history museum to see how the animals find food for their babies;
• a visit to an aquarium to see the different varieties of sea life.

Children can really learn from field trips when adults plan carefully for their success.

*In an educational setting everything we do should support one of our goals for the program.*

# Age Level Developmentally Appropriate Activities

| Page | Activity | Ages | Creative Art | Health-Safety | Language | Large-muscle | Math | Music | Nature-Science | Small-muscle | Social-Emotional | Social Studies | Thinking |
|---|---|---|---|---|---|---|---|---|---|---|---|---|---|
| | **CELEBRATIONS** | | | | | | | | | | | | |
| 18 | Action Prayer | 2–6 | | | | | | | | | • | | |
| 15 | A Birthday Celebration | 2–6 | | | | | • | | | | • | | |
| 14 | Brother/Sister Celebration | 4–6 | | | | | | | | | • | | |
| 13 | Greeting Card Puzzles | 3–6 | | | • | | | | | • | | • | |
| 16 | Happy Toothday | 5–6 | | | | | | • | | | • | | |
| 17 | Love One Another | 4–6 | | | | • | | | | | • | | |
| 12 | Special Guest Day | 3–6 | | | | | | | | • | • | | |
| | **CREATIVE ART** | | | | | | | | | | | | |
| 33 | Berry Pretty Printing | 2–6 | • | | | | | | | • | | • | |
| 34 | Bubble Painting | 2–6 | • | | | | | | | | | | |
| 19 | Coffee Filter Butterflies | 4–6 | • | | | | | | | • | | | |
| 35 | Corncob Printing | 2–6 | • | | | | | | • | | | • | |
| 20 | Exploration Box | 2–6 | | | | | | | | | • | | • |
| 21 | Fancy Feet Collage | 3–6 | • | | • | | | | | • | | | |
| 32 | Feelings Banner | 2–6 | | | | | | | | | • | | • |
| 22 | Flowers at Hand | 2–6 | • | | | | | | | • | | | |
| 36 | Foot Fun | 4–6 | | | • | | | | | • | | | |
| 37 | Gadget Painting | 2–6 | • | | | | | | | • | | | |
| 30 | Greeting Card Mobile | 4–6 | • | | • | | | | | • | | | |
| 23 | Hearts in Our Hands | 5–6 | • | | | | | | | | • | | |
| 24 | Jack-in-the-Box | 4–6 | | | • | • | • | | | | | | |
| 29 | Make Crayons for Rubbings | 3–6 | • | | | | | | | • | | | |
| 39 | Nipa Hut Mosaic | 4–6 | • | | | | | | | • | | • | |
| 42 | Paper Bag Puppets | 4–6 | • | | • | | | | | • | | | |
| 25 | Rainy Day Fun | 2–6 | | | | | | | • | • | | | |
| 26 | Sand Paperweights | 3–6 | • | | | | | | | | • | | |
| 40 | Snip Art Mosaics | 3–5 | • | | | | | | | • | | | • |
| 38 | Spring With a Blue Wash | 4–6 | • | | | | | | • | • | | | |
| 41 | Tissue Paper Butterfly | 4–6 | • | | | | | | • | • | | | |
| 43 | Tube Sock Puppet | 4–6 | • | | • | | | | | | • | | |
| 31 | Underwater Mobile | 4–6 | • | | | | | | | • | | | • |
| 44 | Weaving Box | 4–6 | • | | | | | | | • | | | |
| 27 | Wind Chimes | 4–6 | | | | | | | • | | | | • |
| 28 | Window Hangings | 3–6 | • | | | | | | | | | | • |
| | **FOOD** | | | | | | | | | | | | |
| 49 | The Apple Tree | 2–6 | | | • | | | | • | | | | |
| 50 | Banana Bites | 4–6 | | • | | | | | | | • | | |
| 63 | Butter Shake | 4–6 | | | | | | | • | | • | | |
| 64 | Can Eat—Can't Eat | 2–6 | | • | | | | | | | | | • |
| 55 | Crispy Cheese Animals | 2–6 | | • | | | | | | | • | | |
| 48 | Doughnuts | 3–6 | | • | | | | | | | • | | |
| 47 | Easy Fudge | 4–6 | | | • | | • | | | | • | | |
| 59 | Farmer's Haystacks | 2–6 | | | | | | | | • | • | | |
| 65 | Feed Dorothy | 4–6 | | • | • | | | | | | | | |
| 45 | Friendly Grahams | 2–6 | | | • | | | | | | • | | |

# Age Level Developmentally Appropriate Activities
(continued)

| Page | Activity | Ages | Creative Art | Health-Safety | Language | Large-muscle | Math | Music | Nature-Science | Small-muscle | Social-Emotional | Social Studies | Thinking |
|---|---|---|---|---|---|---|---|---|---|---|---|---|---|
| 60 | Friendship Soup | 2–6 | | • | | | | | | | • | | |
| 51 | Fruit Basket | 3–6 | | | | | | | • | | | | • |
| 52 | Fruit Salad Bar | 3–6 | | • | | | • | | | • | | | |
| 58 | Make Peanut Butter | 3–6 | | • | | | | | • | | | | |
| 56 | Math Trail Mix | 4–6 | | • | • | | • | | | | | | |
| 57 | Mini Pizzas | 3–6 | | | | | | | | | • | | • |
| 46 | Name Sandwiches | 5–6 | | | | | | | | • | | | • |
| 61 | One-Potato, Two-Potatoes | 4–6 | | | | • | • | | | | | | |
| 66 | Picnic Play | 2–6 | | • | | | | | | | • | | |
| 62 | Rice Salad | 3–6 | | • | | | • | | | | | | |
| 54 | Shake a Pudding | 2–6 | | | | | • | | • | | | | |
| 53 | Sugarless Applesauce | 4–6 | | • | | | • | | | | • | | |
| 67 | Taste Treat | 2–6 | | • | | | | | | | | • | |
| 68 | Tidbit Tasting | 3–6 | | • | | | | | | | | • | |
| | **GAMES** | | | | | | | | | | | | |
| 83 | Balance Beam | 2–6 | | | | • | | | | | • | | |
| 69 | Ball and Box Roll | 2–3 | | | | • | | | | | • | | |
| 84 | Beanbag Toss | 2–6 | | | | • | | | | | • | | |
| 70 | Blowing Game | 4–6 | | | | | | | • | | • | | |
| 86 | Clothesline Game | 3–6 | | | | | | | | • | | | • |
| 87 | Do What I Do | 2–6 | | | | | | | | | • | | • |
| 73 | Find the Clock | 2–6 | | | | | | | • | | • | | |
| 77 | Find the Place | 4–6 | | | • | | • | | | | | | • |
| 88 | Laundry Day | 4–6 | | | | | • | | | | | | • |
| 89 | Letter Carrier | 5–6 | | | • | | | | | | | | • |
| 71 | Musical Carpet Squares | 3–6 | | | | • | | | | | • | | |
| 78 | My Right Side Is Vacant | 4–6 | | | • | | | | | | | | • |
| 74 | Name Game | 4–6 | | | • | | | | | | • | | |
| 90 | Pack-a-Toy | 4–6 | | | • | | | | | | | | • |
| 79 | Play "I Want a Friend" | 4–6 | | | | • | | | | | • | | |
| 72 | Push-Croquet | 2–6 | | | | • | | | | | • | | |
| 91 | Season Adventure | 2–6 | | | | • | | | | | | • | |
| 92 | Smelling Game | 3–6 | | | | | | | • | | • | | |
| 80 | Sort the Children | 2–6 | | | | | | | | | • | | • |
| 85 | Walk the Plank | 2–6 | | | | • | | | | | • | | |
| 93 | What Do You Hear? | 4–6 | | | | | | | • | | | | • |
| 76 | What Is It? | 4–6 | | | • | | | | | | | | • |
| 75 | What Is the Number? | 3–5 | | | | | • | | | | | | • |
| 94 | What's That Sound? | 4–6 | | | • | | | | | | | | • |
| 81 | Who Has the Shoe? | 4–6 | | | | | | | | | • | | |
| 82 | Who Is Missing? | 2–6 | | | | | | | | | • | | • |
| | **HOLIDAYS** | | | | | | | | | | | | |
| 110 | Abe Lincoln's Cabin | 5–6 | | | | • | | | | | | • | |
| 117 | Arbor Day Fun | 2–6 | • | | | | | | • | | | | |
| 114 | Bunny Salad | 2–6 | | | | | | | | | • | | • |
| 98 | Christmas Star | 5–6 | | | | | | | • | | | • | |

| Page | Activity | Ages | Creative Art | Health-Safety | Language | Large-muscle | Math | Music | Nature-Science | Small-muscle | Social-Emotional | Social Studies | Thinking |
|---|---|---|---|---|---|---|---|---|---|---|---|---|---|
| 113 | Easter Bunny Card | 3–6 | • | | | | | | | • | | | |
| 111 | Easy Cherry Crisp | 4–6 | | | | | • | | | | • | | |
| 118 | Ecology Worship Center | 2–6 | | | • | | | | | • | | | |
| 119 | Fancy Soaps | 2–4 | | | | | | | | • | • | | |
| 120 | Fourth of July Parfaits | 3–6 | | | | | | | | • | • | | |
| 106 | Friendship Mural | 4–6 | | | • | | | | | | | | |
| 107 | Hello, Mr. Groundhog! | 4–6 | | | • | | | | • | | | | |
| 95 | Indian Symbols | 3–6 | | | | | | | | | | • | • |
| 115 | Make an Easter Egg | 2–6 | • | | | | | | | • | | | |
| 116 | Maypole Dance | 4–6 | | | | • | | • | | | | | |
| 99 | Mexican Ornament | 3–6 | • | | | | | | | • | | | |
| 100 | Mitten Christmas Tree | 2–6 | | | | | | | | | • | | • |
| 105 | New Year's Balloon | 2–6 | • | | • | | | | | | | | |
| 112 | Palm Sunday Parade | 2–6 | | | | • | | • | | | | | |
| 96 | The Pumpkin Patch | 3–6 | • | | | | | | | | | | • |
| 101 | Reindeer Sandwiches | 3–6 | | • | | | | | | | | | |
| 102 | Star Parade | 2–6 | | | | | | • | | | | • | |
| 103 | Straw Ornaments | 5–6 | | | | | | | | • | • | | |
| 97 | A Thanksgiving Litany | 3–6 | | | • | | | | | | | | • |
| 108 | Three Little Valentines | 3–6 | | | | | | | | | • | • | |
| 109 | Valentine Sandwiches | 4–6 | | | | | | | | • | • | | |
| 104 | Wall Christmas Tree | 2–6 | | | | | • | | | • | | | |
| | **LET'S PRETEND** | | | | | | | | | | | | |
| 122 | Baby Birds | 3–6 | | | | • | | • | | | | | |
| 143 | Be a Painter | 2–4 | | | | • | | | | | | • | |
| 144 | Be a Pizza Cook | 2–6 | | | • | | | | | | • | | |
| 128 | Beach Day | 3–6 | | • | | | | | | | | | • |
| 136 | Big Box Cave | 2–6 | | | • | | | | | | • | | |
| 121 | Bird Naps | 2–6 | | | | | | | • | | • | | |
| 123 | Caring for Pets | 3–6 | | | | | | | • | | • | | |
| 137 | Changing Seasons | 2–6 | | | | | | • | • | | | | |
| 129 | Family Barbecue | 4–6 | | | | | | | | | • | | • |
| 141 | Fishing Game | 5–6 | | | • | | | | | | • | | |
| 124 | Fly Away | 3–6 | | | | | | | • | | | | |
| 130 | Gift Boxes | 4–6 | | | • | | | | • | | | | |
| 140 | Make Car Repairs | 2–6 | | | | | | | | • | • | | • |
| 125 | Mother Hen | 2–6 | | | | | | | • | | | | • |
| 126 | Move Like an Animal | 3–6 | | | | • | | • | | | | | |
| 142 | Moving Day | 3–6 | | | | | | | | | • | • | |
| 131 | My Place | 2–6 | | | | | | | | | • | | |
| 132 | "Needlepoint" | 5–6 | | | | | | | | • | | • | |
| 133 | Safety Play | 4–6 | | • | • | | | | | | | | • |
| 145 | Sailing Boats | 2–6 | | | | | | | | | | • | • |
| 127 | Scarf Butterfly | 4–6 | | | • | | | | | | | | • |
| 134 | Scrub-a-Dub | 2–6 | | • | | | | | | | • | | |
| 146 | Shoe Repair Shop | 2–6 | | | • | | | | | • | | | |

# Age Level Developmentally Appropriate Activities

(continued)

| Page | Activity | Ages | Creative Art | Health-Safety | Language | Large-muscle | Math | Music | Nature-Science | Small-muscle | Social-Emotional | Social Studies | Thinking |
|---|---|---|---|---|---|---|---|---|---|---|---|---|---|
| 135 | Sleepover | 3–6 | | | | | | | | | • | | |
| 138 | Tent Play | 2–6 | | | • | | | | | | • | | |
| 139 | Weather Game | 2–6 | | | • | | | | • | | | | |
| | **MUSIC** | | | | | | | | | | | | |
| 152 | Act out the Song "Rocking" | 2–4 | | | | | | • | | | • | | |
| 155 | Ankle Bell Dance | 2–6 | | | | • | | • | | | | • | |
| 157 | Bamboo Plate Dance | 5–6 | | | | • | | • | | | | | |
| 164 | Beach Fun | 3–6 | | | | • | | • | | | | | |
| 147 | Body Parts | 2–6 | | | | • | | • | | | | | |
| 156 | Butterflies | 2–6 | | | | • | | • | • | | | | |
| 158 | Circle Dancing | 5–6 | | | | | | • | | | • | | |
| 148 | Clap a Song | 3–6 | | | | • | | • | | | | | |
| 151 | Creation Parade | 2–6 | | | | | | • | | | | | • |
| 165 | Echo Songs | 3–6 | | | • | | | • | | | | | |
| 171 | Express Praise | 2–5 | | | | • | | • | | | | | |
| 163 | A Friend Loves | 3–6 | | | • | | | • | | | | | |
| 159 | Having Fun Today | 2–6 | | | | | | • | | | • | | • |
| 166 | I Am First | 2–3 | | | | | | • | | | • | | |
| 160 | Musical Puddles | 2–4 | | | | | | • | | | • | | |
| 149 | Pass the Present | 5–6 | | | | | | • | | | • | | • |
| 161 | Play Londonbashi | 3–6 | | | | | | • | | | | | |
| 168 | Rainbow Song | 2–4 | | | | | | • | • | | | | |
| 170 | The Recycle Band | 4–6 | | | | | | • | • | | | | |
| 169 | Ring the Bells | 2–4 | | | | | | • | | | | | |
| 153 | Scarf/Streamer Dancing | 3–6 | | | | | | • | | | | | |
| 172 | Show Love | 4–6 | | | | | | • | | | | | |
| 154 | Swinging Song | 2–6 | | | | | | • | | | | | |
| 162 | Tiptoe, Shhh! | 2–6 | | | | | | • | | | | | |
| 167 | Welcome, Friend | 3–6 | | | | | | • | | | | | |
| 150 | Yes, I Can | 2–4 | | | | | | • | | | | | |
| | **NATURE** | | | | | | | | | | | | |
| 174 | Beauty Spot | 4–6 | | | • | | | | • | | | | |
| 185 | Bug Catchers | 4–6 | | | | | | | • | | | | • |
| 186 | The Butterfly Cycle | 4–6 | | | | | | | • | • | | | |
| 175 | Ceiling Stars | 2–6 | | | • | | | | • | | | | |
| 182 | A Classroom Seasonal Tree | 2–6 | | | | | | | • | | | | • |
| 173 | Concentration | 5–6 | | | • | | | | • | | | | |
| 187 | Crazy Caterpillars | 3–6 | • | | | | | | • | | | | |
| 176 | Discover the Good Earth | 5–6 | | | | | | | • | | | | • |
| 190 | A Discovery Museum | 2–6 | | | | | | | • | | • | | |
| 177 | Don't Pollute | 2–6 | | | • | | | | • | | | | |
| 188 | Earthworm Day | 2–6 | | | | | | | • | | | | |
| 189 | Firefly Lights | 2–6 | | | • | | | | • | | | | |
| 178 | Gardening Movement | 4–6 | | | | • | | | • | | | | |
| 193 | Here Comes the Wind | 2–6 | | | | | | | • | | • | | |
| 191 | Living Things Change | 3–6 | | | | | | | • | | | | • |

# Age Level Developmentally Appropriate Activities

(continued)

| Page | Activity | Ages | Creative Art | Health-Safety | Language | Large-muscle | Math | Music | Nature-Science | Small-muscle | Social-Emotional | Social Studies | Thinking |
|------|----------|------|:---:|:---:|:---:|:---:|:---:|:---:|:---:|:---:|:---:|:---:|:---:|
| 192 | Matching Game | 5–6 | | | | | | | • | • | | | • |
| 194 | Nature Patterns | 4–6 | | | | | • | | • | | | | • |
| 179 | Pine-cone Tray | 5–6 | • | | | | | | • | • | | | |
| 180 | Plant Seeds | 2–6 | | | | | | | • | • | | | |
| 195 | Ribbon Mobile | 3–6 | | | | | | | • | • | | | |
| 181 | Save Our Earth | 4–6 | | | | | | | • | | | | • |
| 196 | Soak It Up! | 3–6 | | | | | | | • | | | | • |
| 183 | Space Play | 3–6 | | | • | | | | • | | | | |
| 184 | Take a Wonder Walk | 2–6 | | | | • | | | • | | | | • |
| 197 | Weather Suitcase | 2–6 | | | | | | | • | | | | • |
| | **PEOPLE TO SEE** | | | | | | | | | | | | |
| 199 | A Doctor or Nurse Visits | 2–6 | | • | | | | | | | | • | • |
| 203 | Invite a Police Officer | 2–6 | | • | | | | | | | | • | |
| 200 | Persons With Handicaps | 4–6 | | | | | | | | | • | • | |
| 202 | An Unusual Job | 3–6 | | | • | | | | | | | • | |
| 201 | Visit a Potter | 4–6 | • | | | | | | | • | | | |
| 204 | Visit a Weaver | 4–6 | • | | | | | | | • | | | |
| 198 | Visit With a Dentist | 3–6 | | • | | | | | | | • | | |
| | **PLACES TO GO** | | | | | | | | | | | | |
| 206 | Fast Food Field Trip | 3–6 | | | | | | | | | • | • | |
| 208 | Greenhouse or Nursery | 4–6 | | | | | | | • | | | | |
| 210 | Gymnasium | 3–6 | | • | | • | | | | | | | |
| 211 | Home Building Site | 4–6 | | | | | | | | | | • | |
| 212 | Let's Go Shopping | 3–6 | | | • | | | | | | | | • |
| 216 | Pet Store | 3–6 | | | | | | | • | | • | | |
| 217 | Picnic Echo Chant | 2–6 | | | • | | | | | | | | • |
| 218 | Pizza Parlor | 4–6 | | • | | | | | | | | • | |
| 219 | Recycle Center | 3–6 | | | | | | | | | | • | • |
| 205 | Vegetable or Fruit Market | 4–6 | | • | | | | | | | | • | |
| 207 | Visit a Fire Station | 4–6 | | • | | | | | | | | • | |
| 209 | Visit a Grocery Store | 4–6 | | | • | | | | | | | • | |
| 213 | Visit a Newspaper | 5–6 | | | • | | | | | | | • | |
| 214 | Visit an Orchard | 4–6 | | | • | | | | | | | • | |
| 215 | Visit a Paint Store | 4–6 | | | | | | | • | | • | | |
| 220 | Visit a School Band | 4–6 | | | | | | • | | | | | • |
| | **STORYTELLING** | | | | | | | | | | | | |
| 221 | Basket or Bag Story | 3–6 | | | • | | | | | | | | • |
| 233 | Bible Drama | 4–6 | | | | | | | | | • | | • |
| 234 | Box Theater | 4–6 | | | • | | | | | | | | • |
| 236 | Character Cards | 4–6 | | | • | | | | | | • | | |
| 237 | Classifying Seasonal Words | 4–6 | | | • | | | | | | | | • |
| 238 | Do You Remember? | 5–6 | | | • | | | | | | | | • |
| 243 | Experience a Poem | 5–6 | • | | • | | | | | | | | |
| 222 | Flannelboard Story | 2–6 | | | • | | | | | | | | • |
| 223 | Hand Talk | 2–6 | | | • | | | | | | | | • |
| 224 | Magnetic Board Stories | 4–6 | | | • | | | | | | | | • |

# Age Level Developmentally Appropriate Activities

(continued)

| Page | Activity | Ages | Creative Art | Health-Safety | Language | Large-muscle | Math | Music | Nature-Science | Small-muscle | Social-Emotional | Social Studies | Thinking |
|---|---|---|---|---|---|---|---|---|---|---|---|---|---|
| 225 | Microphone Talk | 3–6 | | | • | | | | | | • | | |
| 226 | Mixed-up Stories | 4–6 | | | • | | | | | | | | • |
| 240 | Noah's Ark | 2–6 | | | • | | | | • | | | | |
| 242 | Oral Rebus Stories | 2–4 | | | • | | | | | | | | • |
| 245 | Our Book | 4–6 | | | • | | | | | | | | • |
| 227 | Participation Stories | 2–6 | | | • | | | | | | | | |
| 241 | A Philippine Legend | 2–6 | | | • | | | | • | | | • | |
| 244 | Problem-solver Puppet | 2–6 | | | • | | | | | | • | | |
| 228 | Retelling With Art | 5–6 | • | | • | | | | | | | | • |
| 229 | Sing a Story | 2–6 | | | • | | | • | | | | | |
| 231 | Stories With Sound Effects | 2–6 | | | • | | | | | | | | • |
| 230 | Story Box | 2–6 | | | • | | | | | | | | • |
| 239 | Story Sequencing | 5–6 | | | • | | | | | | | | • |
| 232 | Storybook Friend | 2–6 | | | • | | | | | | • | | |
| 235 | Talking a Story | 5–6 | | | • | | | | | | | | • |

# Index to Christian Values

**BIBLE**
Learn some Bible background, 63, 104, 112, 169

**CHRISTIAN HERITAGE**
Learn background of holidays, 98, 104, 112, 113
Learn symbols, stories, and traditions, 98, 99, 102, 113, 115, 120, 148, 222, 224, 230, 233, 240
Participate in customs of holidays, 98, 100, 103, 169
Value our own and community traditions, 104, 224

**CREATION**
**Being Good Stewards**
Care for God's world through recycling, 181
Help preserve the world for now and the future, 118, 121, 178, 181, 182, 216, 219
Respect and care for all of God's creation, 24, 28, 29, 33, 35, 66, 117, 118, 121, 122, 123, 126, 162, 170, 177, 179, 180, 183, 185, 219

**Understanding God's Creation**
Appreciate the wonder and beauty of God's world, 19, 22, 27, 124, 141, 176, 178, 184, 190, 196, 208
Learn about God's plan for changing seasons, 38, 91, 107, 137, 182, 195, 197
Observe and examine events in the natural world, 25, 30, 49, 54, 70, 92, 93, 94, 114, 117, 134, 139, 141, 151, 168, 173, 175, 183, 186, 187, 188, 193, 194, 196

**GOD**
**Responding to God**
Appreciate/discover the wonders of God's world, 20, 31, 41, 63, 68, 96, 107, 114, 121, 123, 124, 128, 137, 164, 170, 186, 188, 189, 194, 214
Build trust in God, 38, 135, 175
Celebrate God's plan for growth and change, 15, 16, 27, 28, 40, 49, 137, 149, 156, 180, 191, 208, 225
Enjoy participating in celebrations, 13, 100, 102, 104, 112, 115, 148.
Experience joy and fun in praising God, 30, 39, 97, 116, 127, 150, 153, 154, 165, 169, 171, 191, 215
Give thanksgiving for food and shelter, 51, 61, 64, 65
Know God is with us and loves and cares for us, 67,

# Index